Verolanium Urbs Britannico=
Romana a Voadicia Icenorum
Regina Sub Nerone
excisa fuit.
Ordinibus alternis.
Scala Pedum
Via Hemstediam ducens
Southgate
Muri Antiqui Reliquiæ
Vestigia
Cavitas
pedestris
Heic Porta olim fuisse videtur
VERO LA NIVM
AN TI QVUM
Vestigia
Umbra
Umbra Strati
Strati
Trames du-
cens ad Gorham
bury Villam olim
Vicecomitis
Verolamij.
Domus
Parochi
nunc Arva &
Pascua
Pars Muri adhuc
restans Gorhamblock
nuncupata
Via Regia ad
Redburn
Non longe hinc
Prioratus Sta
Mariæ de pratis
Colne Fluvius
Hill
Scala Pedum

The New Book of St Albans 1976
has been published as a
Limited Edition of which
this is

Number 306

A complete list of the
original subscribers is
printed at the back of
the book

THE NEW BOOK OF ST ALBANS

FRONT COVER: St Albans, from a 19th century print.

The Clock Tower

THE NEW BOOK OF ST ALBANS

AN ILLUSTRATED RECORD

BY

DR ELSIE TOMS MA PhD

BARRACUDA BOOKS LIMITED
CHESHAM, BUCKINGHAMSHIRE, ENGLAND
MCMLXXVI

PUBLISHED BY BARRACUDA BOOKS LIMITED

CHESHAM, ENGLAND

AND PRINTED BY

MALCOLM G. READ LIMITED

175 BERMONDSEY STREET

LONDON SE1

BOUND BY

BOOKBINDERS OF LONDON LIMITED

LONDON N5

JACKET PRINTED BY

WHITE CRESCENT PRESS LIMITED

LUTON, ENGLAND

LITHOGRAPHY BY

SOUTH MIDLANDS LITHO PLATES LIMITED

LUTON, ENGLAND

TYPE SET IN

MONOTYPE BASKERVILLE SERIES 169

BY SOUTH BUCKS TYPESETTERS LIMITED

BEACONSFIELD, ENGLAND

ISBN 0 86023 019 8

Contents

Acknowledgements

Many people and organisations have contributed to this illustrated record and thanks are due to them all. In particular the City, Abbey and Museum authorities, as well as the Verulamium Museum have helped throughout its preparation with advice, information and the loan of illustrative material.

Lord Verulam and the Bishop of St Albans have lent their encouragement and interest, and each has kindly placed this on record on the opposite page.

Thanks are also due to the Corporation of the City and District of St Albans for permission to reproduce charters and minutes, to St Albans Central Library for material and to Mr Keyte and Miss Wells for their help and the reservation facilities, to Verulamium Museum for a number of illustrations, to the Herts Advertiser, National Gallery, Trinity College Library, Dublin, British Library, and Gorhambury Collection through the Earl of Verulam, for illustrations and to the St Albans and West Herts Archaeological Society and The Fraternity of the Friends of St Albans Abbey for informing members of the limited edition, and to local and county newspapers for their public support for this project.

(Note: The author's illness during the final stages of preparation of this book may have inadvertently caused the omission of proper acknowledgments, formal or otherwise. The publishers wish to apologise for any such omissions, and assure all who have helped of the author's appreciation.)

Foreword

by the Earl of Verulam

Perhaps no history of St Albans has been more popularly received and widely acclaimed than that written by Dr Elsie Toms in 1962. This present volume is complementary to that history for in addition to a concise and readable record of the city, it shows in pictures some of the welath of ancient buildings that still remain for the visitor to St Albans to enjoy.

Archaeological evidence shows that man has lived at St Albans for more than two thousand years. Dr Elsie Toms takes us from Roman times to the present day with the authority of a major historian and with the special insight of one who has been Mayoress of the City of St Albans.

The City has retained its historic character but has moved with the times. Side by side we have modern development, the remains of the Roman City of Verulamium, buildings of the Middle Ages, and the Cathedral itself.

For the visitor to St Albans this book is the ideal souvenir. No one but an expert, such as Dr Elsie Toms, could have compiled so comprehensive a pictorial study of the City and I am delighted that she should have invited me to write this Foreword.

GORHAMBURY,
ST ALBANS.
August, 1976

Verulam.

Preface

By the Right Reverend The Bishop of St Albans

Cities, just like families and nations, need a story which will help to explain how they have developed and sum up what they stand for. A story builds a mass of people into a community which has a personality of its own. This is not just a luxury, since a feeling of belonging and loyalty to the community can help a person to go beyond his interests as an individual to recognise the responsibility we all have for our neighbours.

The vitality of this community spirit is threatened by changes that are obvious to all. Towns grow larger and if they are near to London, or some other great centre, become little more than dormitories. There is more moving around and fewer people stay to live where they were born and bred. Many people seem to remain strangers all their lives having only weak links with the local community. They do not know and so do not feel part of the story of the place in which they live.

There is a danger of something vital being lost here. I believe that all of us who are citizens of St Albans owe a great debt of gratitude to Dr Elsie Toms for telling the story of our town with so much love and humour. The success of her previous book will ensure a warm welcome for this new revised work, a briefer account but enriched by a generous number of well chosen illustrations. I hope that it will help us all to a greater appreciation of what we daily see around us and so make us more conscious of belonging to a community which has achieved much in the past and which needs our loyalty and active concern if it is to have a worthwhile future.

ABBEY GATE HOUSE,
August, 1976.

Robert St. Albans

The Ruines of Time

I was that Citie, which the garland wore
Of Britaines pride, delivered unto me
By Romane Victors, which it wonne of yore;
Though nought at all but ruines now I bee,
And lye in mine owne ashes as ye see:
Verlame I was; what bootes it that I was
Sith now I am but weedes and wastfull grass?

O Rome thy ruine I lament and rue,
And in thy fall my fatall overthrowe,
That whilom was, whilst heavens with equal vowe
Deigned to behold me, and their gifts bestowe,
The picture of thy pride in pompous shew;
And of the whole world as thou wast the Empresse,
So I of this small Northerne world was Princesse.
To tell the beawtie of my buildings fayre,
Adorned with purest golde, and precious stone;

High towers, faire temples, goodly theaters,
Strong walls, rich porches, princelie pallaces,
Large streetes, brave houses, sacred sepulchers,
Sure gates, sweete gardens, stately galleries.
Wrought with faire pillours, and fine imageries
All these (O pitie) now are turned to dust,
And overgrowen with blacke oblivions rust.

Edmund Spenser.

City Heritage

It is sad to contemplate the paucity of histories of St Albans, surely the town with more history than most—we have so much because we have had more time than most to make it. From prehistoric times until the present day, things have happened here which have had their effect far beyond our boundaries. In how many cities has any document influenced the law-courts of the world as Magna Carta has done? Yet we heard it first in St Albans in 1213. The Royal Society has influenced the scientific thinking of much of the world—the trends of thought which led to its foundation can be said to have descended from a book by our St Albans thinker, Francis Bacon's 'Novum Organum'. Agricultural authorities of the world ask advice from Rothamsted Experimental Station at Harpenden, founded by a local landowner. Ships from almost any port in the world send chronometers which need repair to St Albans. The third printing press in this country was set up in St Albans in the fifteenth century, and St Albans still goes on printing.

The City and District of St Albans cannot be accused of being behind the times, for it is in the forefront of the movement for conservation. We should like to have conserved more, but the town planning acts were not passed early enough to save some worthwhile features. Even so, the Department of the Environment list some hundreds of our buildings which connoisseurs consider worth preserving, and any threat to one of these lets loose a torrent of protest. History lovers, we do really do our best to save for your descendants the heritage of the past.

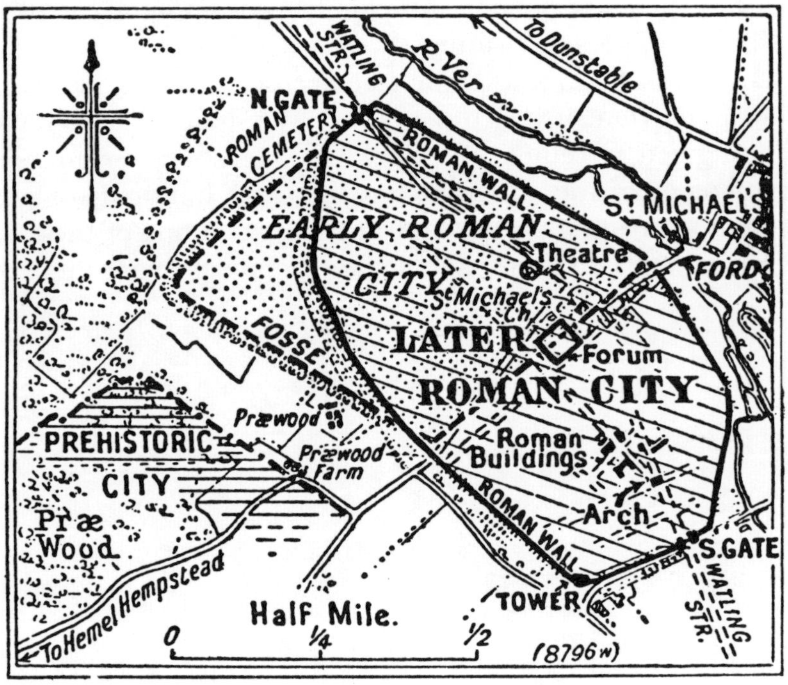

ABOVE: Ford on River Ver. Prehistoric route to Belgic and Roman Verulamium.

BELOW: Map of the Belgic and first Roman and later Verulamiums.

Verulamium

The neighbourhood of St Albans was inhabited long ago. Stone Age Man has certainly left his mark, and his stone axes and arrowheads, primitive pottery and other artifacts of far-off days are now in the Museum. But the real history of the district starts with the coming of the Belgic tribes from the Continent. The Catuvellauni settled and became dominant in Hertfordshire, Essex and the neighbouring area. A 'Celtic metropolis,' (as Mortimer Wheeler called it), was established in the valley of the River Ver, based on the ford over the river now marked by St Michael's Bridge. These settlers were far from being the savages described by some Roman writers. In the course of the first century BC the chief stronghold was at Wheathampstead, but it moved to the neighbourhood of St Albans about 15 BC, and at the time of the first invasion of Julius Caesar (55 BC) there was a trackway to Colchester, by AD 10 the Celtic centre. The Wheathampstead stronghold remains are known as Devil's Dyke and the Slad, and the dyke called Beech Bottom, lies between there and St Albans. The British leader was Cassivelaunus, with whom Caesar found it necessary to negotiate, since he proved a more formidable opponent than expected. Although Britain did not immediately become a Roman province, from that time there was a growing connection with the Roman world, and the Belgae were the first tribes in Britain to mint coins. They were of gold, silver and copper, and many coin-moulds were left here. As there were then no written British characters, the Britons borrowed Roman letters to strike their inscriptions on the coins, and thus we know the abbreviated names of the British ruler—TASC, for Tasciovanus, and VER or VERL for Verlam, the latter name being taken over by the Romans, with an inserted 'r' to make it easier for Latin-speaking tongues to pronounce. They added the more familiar '-ium'. But the old pronunciation has survived some 2000 years, and 'Verlam Road' may still be heard on the lips of old St Albans inhabitants. The greatest of the leaders of the Catuvellauni was Cunobolin, son of Tasciovanus, and Verulam became the capital.

In the interval between the Roman invasions of 55 BC and AD 43, there was a considerable growth of trade between Britain and the Roman Empire, and many Britons grew familiar with the Latin language and the polyglot mass of Roman travellers and later soldiers. It is not surprising that this part of the country submitted with much less resistance than the tribes farther west and north. In fact, Hertfordshire, as we now know it, submitted remarkably soon, with the result that the town, according to Tacitus, was given the title of 'municipium', and the great main-road of Watling Street was early in construction. There does not appear to have been a garrison of soldiers stationed there for more than five years. Sheppard Frere found an enclosure which is believed to be a military encampment, but it may have been a camp for navvies, working on Watling Street, and unconnected with military uses, which had ceased in the area by AD 49.

Romanisation proceeded rapidly, and the Belgic town was being replaced by a Roman one on a slightly different site, when in AD 61 the builders of Roman rule suffered a sharp set-back. Matters in East Anglia had not gone on as peaceably as at Verulamium, and the Iceni, led by Boudicca, widow of their chief, rose in revolt. They attacked Colchester, and destroyed it, then moved on to London, an important trading-post. They next attacked Verulamium and burnt it. The marks of burnt debris can be seen to this day.

Boudicca was followed northwards, defeated and executed, and rebuilding must have started immediately. The first Roman city had been built largely of wood, and much of the 2nd city must have been of the same material, but more and more brick and flint became the house-material and the improvement in the quality and design of the city brought sophistication and beauty. Large houses with gardens and bath-wings, with heating arrangements, and underfloor ducts for the circulation of hot air, (hypocausts) were a forerunner of modern underfloor central heating. The authorities were anxious to see the city rise rapidly, and encouraged building, giving assistance to local people who wanted housing. It is reported that the Roman governor made personal gifts towards this end, and architects and craftsmen must also have been called upon for their skills.

By AD 79 the main lines of streets and many shops and other buildings were in use. The massive structure of the Forum had risen, just at the crossroads in the heart of the city. This structure can be dated, for in contrast to our habit of laying foundation stones at the start of a new building, the Romans dedicated the finished edifice, and the inscription on the Forum was dedicated during the governorship of Agricola, who was here *c* 78, and departed *c* AD 80. The Forum contained the law-courts and other local government offices, the public meeting-place with its rostrum for public speakers, a temple, and soon after, a market-hall, on the other side of Watling Street.

Within the next century, there were many developments. Defences were constructed in the form of massive walls, over 20 feet high (substantial portions of which are in charge of the Department of Ancient Monuments). There were four imposing gates: the London Gate, and the Silchester Gate on the SE and SW, and Chestergate with the fourth on the NE side. Between the London Gate and the NE ran the Watling Street, and on it were to be found a triangular temple, the Forum, shops and the Theatre; it formed the 'High Street' of the city. Beyond were the larger houses, quite luxurious, with some of the finest mosaic pavements to be found in this country. The walls of corridors and rooms were plastered and painted, many of them with imitation marbled paint, since there is no marble in the vicinity. One large piece of surviving plaster is a ceiling, put together from several thousands of fragments by the patience of Prof Norman Davey. A length of painted wall plaster shows a frieze of birds and animal heads. This piece was lent to the British Museum for several years after it was found, because it was so big that the Verulamium Museum could not accommodate it until enlarged. The mosaics were magnificent. The small *tesserae* were small cubes of coloured stone, set in patterns in the floors. Among the finest mosaics are the scallop shell (semi-circular), the Sea-god, with a fine pair of lobster-claws in his hair, and another set in the floor of the City Hall (unfortunately hidden by the bar), but the finest of all is the lion, with its victim, a stag with its horns in the lion's jaws. These are all 2nd century, the time of the best building in Verulamium.

The Theatre stood alongside Watling Street, north of the Forum. On the Greek open air style, it had a large orchestra area, with a semicircular stage which was soon enlarged by halving the space, and putting in extra seats. For theatrical shows, the stage curtains were let down into a slot in front of the stage. There were several temples, one just behind the theatre, possibly connected with religious ceremonies. When Christianity began to spread, the Theatre began to die, and it became the town's refuse dump.

There are untold treasures yet to be discovered, when money will allow for more extensive excavation. We have not yet found the public baths, though in such a sophisticated city, they must have been important. Neither have we found the amphitheatre, though it is unlikely to be missing, and in fact is mentioned in chronicles in connection with the martyrdom of St Alban. We know of more than one triumphal arch, one across Watling Street outside the Theatre, and both the others on the line of Watling Street. They are as yet the only ones found in Roman Britain. As these words are written, an aerial survey has shown up the outlines of two further temples, and shops and houses fronting onto Watling Street.

Belgic coin-mould.

ABOVE: Shops of first Roman Verulamium. Pre-Boudiccan—before 60 AD. (Model in Verulamium Museum)

BELOW: Digging up Verulamium.
Coins from Verulamium.

ABOVE: Roman house; Verulamium. (Reconstruction in Museum)

LEFT: Roman helmet.

RIGHT: Two Roman jugs, one glass and one pottery.

LEFT: Hunt Cup—Castor Ware.

RIGHT: Roman saucepan. (Mid 1st cent.)

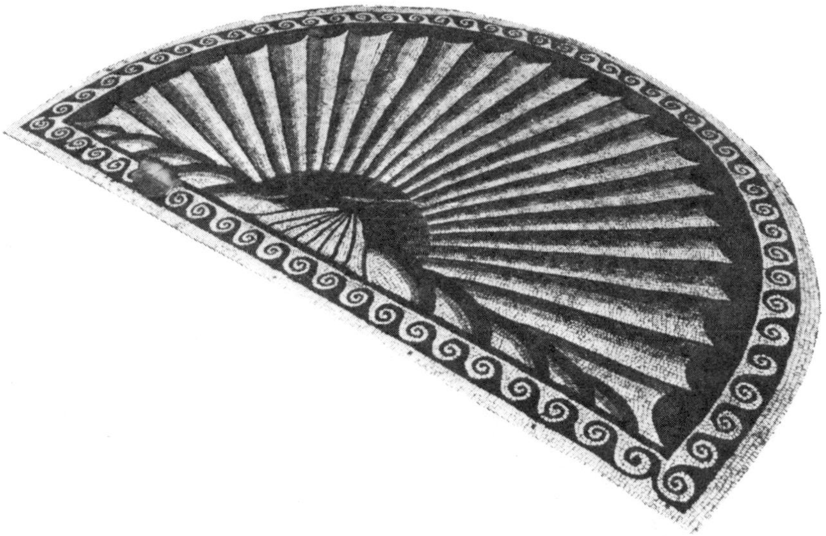

ABOVE: Mosaic, set in floor of City Hall, St Albans.

BELOW: Scallop Shell. (Verulamium Museum)

ABOVE: Reconstruction of Forum, and BELOW: Reconstruction of triangular temple.

Reconstruction of Theatre.

ABOVE: Roman Theatre as it is, Gorhambury.
(Excavated by Dr Kathleen Kenyon)

LEFT: Theatre: stage area, Gorhambury.

RIGHT: Town Wall showing construction, Verulamium Park.

ABOVE: South-east or London Gate.

BELOW: Seagod mosaic, showing lobster claws. (Verulamium—2nd cent.)

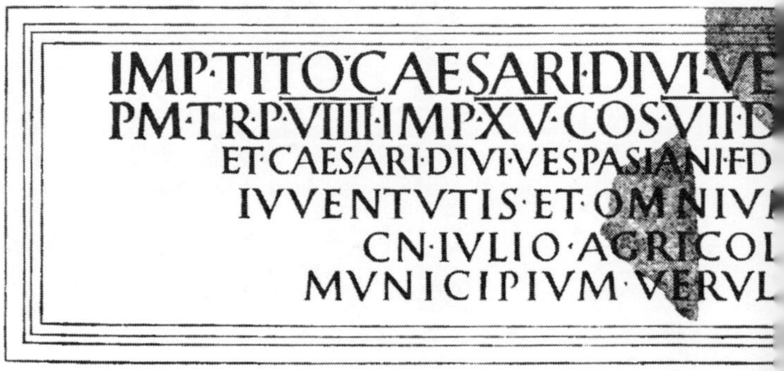

LEFT : Sta

RIGHT : Bronze statuett

CENTRE LEFT : Lion mosai

CENTRE RIGH
(Reconstructe

BELOW : Fragment of
Verulam

animals.

(Museum—2nd cent.)

aws. (Museum—2nd cent.)

plaster ceiling.
rman Davey)

inscription of Forum,
Museum)

ABOVE: Execution of Alban. (Matt. Paris. Permission of Board of Trinity College, Dublin)

BELOW: The Shrine of St Alban. (Matt. Paris. Permission of Board of Trinity College, Dublin)

The First Martyr

When one removes all the legends from the story of St Alban, our own particular saint, two facts seem to stand immovable—there was a man called Alban, and he was executed as a Christian at Verulamium in Roman times. The Romans were tolerant in permitting variations in heterogenous worship, which is natural when one considers the multi-religious nature of the army. The one proviso was that the Deified Emperor should be associated with the other gods. The martyrs were Jewish and Christian, and monogamous, so that their refusal to worship the Emperor took on the aspect of treason. And so we come to St Alban. We know little of him, beyond these bare facts, so the imagination can range from the probable to the downright impossible. To judge the truth of legends is made difficult by the hard fact that the possession of a local saint and martyr was a financial asset to a mediaeval religious House. Incidents were invented and new versions produced to enhance the reputation of the saint and supplement the paucity of proved facts. Hence the eagerness of the monks to 'discover' Saint Amphibalus—a saint who never existed, at least under that name.

The earliest surviving account of the death of Alban is found in the writings of Gildas, a mid-sixth century writer and a West-countryman. Ignorant of this part of the country, he probably drew on some earlier, possibly fourth century version as source, containing some of the legends of the martyrdom, and these were copied by the Venerable Bede, whose account was regarded as definitive until quite recent times. Now it is felt that Bede's date is wrong, and a much earlier date more likely, putting the martyrdom back nearly a century, to about AD 209.

Bede says that it occurred during the persecution under Diocletian, yet giving the later date as fact.

A manuscript at Turin, obviously based on earlier sources than Gildas, gives the name of the Emperor as Severus, who is on record as carrying on a fierce persecution of Christians and Jews in Gaul. In 208 he crossed over to Britain with his two sons, Caracalla and Geta. His main object was to campaign against the northern tribes and he took Caracalla with him, leaving Geta as his representative in the south of Britain. It would seem that Geta was the official who is called 'the judge' by Bede. The earlier date gets over the difficulty that the Diocletian persecution was mainly on the Continent and not in Britain.

The early document would seem to have given a vivid, but imaginative account of the trial of Alban, which is followed by Bede, who places it firmly as having taken place as 'near the city of Verulamium'. Bede speaks of the church erected and in use. He exaggerated its grandeur, and says that it was already a place of pilgrimage, where miracles occurred. The legends which he relates have passed into the generally-told story of the saint. According to his account a Christian priest came to Alban's house by night for refuge, and during the night, he converted his host, who assisted him to escape next day, by disguising him and assuming his guest's cloak. A word meaning cloak was, by ignorance of a scribe or a slip in transcribing the manuscript, attached to the priest as a name, Amphibalus. This was gladly seized on by the later St Albans' monks as a welcome addition to their relics.

Alban was arrested and brought before the judge, who argued with him, and failing to shake his faith, sentenced him to be executed by being torn by wild animals. He later changed his mind, and allowed him the death of a Roman citizen, who was entitled to be beheaded. Probably some bold spirit called Geta's attention to the fact that he had blundered, and so the scene of the martyrdom was hastily removed from the amphitheatre to the top of Holm hurst Hill, where the Abbey still stands. Of course legends gathered round the incidents of the execution. According to Bede the prisoner was led out of the city by the bridge over the river, but the bridge was so crowded that it collapsed, and the spectators were thrown into the river, while Alban continued his journey by the ford next to the bridge, and passed up the hill for some half-mile. As embroidery to the account, it was added that the river dried up so that the saint went over the ford dry-shod, that the original headsman was converted by the fortitude of Alban and refused to execute him, and that his substitute's eyes dropped out. This incident may be seen carved on the pedestal of the shrine, erected in the Abbey in the Saint's Chapel, in the early 14th century.

And so Alban became, not just, as we were wont to believe, the first Christian martyr of Britain, but indeed of Western Europe, and his own countrymen marked their realisation of his position by building a little church in his honour soon after his death. We gather from Gildas that the British Christians built 'basilicas' in honour of their martyrs. Alban would have been an early recipient of this honour, not only in this country but on the Continent, where there are churches dedicated to Alban in places down the Rhone Valley, along the trade-route between Britain and the Mediterranean. And when in the early fifth century, St Germanus, Bishop of Auxerre, came to Britain in answer to a plea to deal with a heresy in this country, he considered Alban sufficiently important for the party to pay a visit to his shrine, which was even then well known.

Later the Dark Ages clamped down on information about events in a large part of Western Europe, but when the curtain lifted, Verulam was no longer a flourishing city. The Saxons had overrun the area, settled, and had become Christians—what a good job the British brides had done in converting their heathen husbands. They founded a village clustered around the little church which had then become the most important building.

So we have good evidence for our claim that Christian worship on this site has never ceased since soon after the death of Alban, and that the Abbey of to-day, with its continuous train of predecessors, must be one of the oldest, if not *the* oldest site of Christian worship in this country. There need be little surprise that when squabbles arose in the twelfth century between the Abbots of Westminster and St Albans, as to which was the premier Abbey of England, Pope Adrian IV (Nicholas Breakspear, son of an Abbey tenant at Abbot's Langley, whose father and uncle were monks in St Albans Abbey) gave his ruling that the title belonged to St Albans. Thus it remained, if only nominally towards the end, until the Dissolution.

ABOVE: Execution of Alban, from pedestal of Shrine.

LEFT: The Shrine, showing feretory on top.

RIGHT: The Pedestal of the Shrine today.

ABOVE: Offa and the building of the Abbey. (Permission of Board of Trinity College, Dublin)

LEFT: Virgin and Child, with kneeling figure of Matt. Paris. (Permission of British Library. Roy. MS)

RIGHT: Offa and his Abbey. (Permission of British Lib. Cott. MS. Nero)

The Great House of God

There is a wonderful manuscript, written and illustrated by the hand of the historian-monk, Matthew Paris (d 1259) in the Library of Trinity College, Dublin. It contains the story of St Alban's martyrdom, an account of the visit of St Germanus, and the legends told of the founding of the Abbey by King Offa of Mercia. The third part of the manuscript gives us the one certain date—Offa founded the monastery by charter in the year 793. That is confirmed by other evidence. Of course, legends have grown up around this dated legal document, and they are but legends. For instance, the tales say that Offa searched for the bones of St Alban because they had been lost, and he 'discovered' them by a miracle. This is nonsense; the bones of St Alban were not lost. Bede, writing about sixty years earlier, says that there was a church at St Albans to which pilgrims travelled, and at which miracles were observed, and where there must have been a service of custodian-priests. Offa probably regularised the organisation, and placed it under the Benedictine Rule, but we know no more, though legend says, quite plausibly, that the first Abbot was a kinsman of Offa.

After this, we know little of the early Saxon Abbots. Not until the translation of Abbot Alfric II to the Archbishopric of Canterbury in 990, do we get a definite date, though tradition gives 948 for Abbot Ulsinus, who is said to have founded the three churches, St Peter's, St Michael's, and St Stephen's, and also the weekly market. Matthew Paris tells us that he built houses at his own expense, and helped settlers with money and materials—a foretaste of the modern housing and planning committees—our first town-planner.

The struggle of the country against the Danes was reflected at St Albans. The Northmen came to Hertfordshire, as is remembered in local place names such as Dane End and the name Dacorum for one of the old Hundreds. St Albans had a small royal fort (Kingsbury) about this time—possibly one of the military posts of Alfred the Great. The remains of part of its dry moat form a children's small playingfield in New England Street. This borough had a civilian population who earned a living cultivating fish in a large fishpool, between Kingsbury Hill and the ruins of the north part of Verulamium, and there were constant quarrels between the Abbey and Kingsbury, each jealous of the other, and each hurling charges of oppression against the other. Abbot Alfric bought from King Edgar the Peaceable permission to drain the lake, and so destroyed the livelihood of the citizens of Kingsbury. Some thereupon deserted their homes, swelling the population of St Albans, and others became outlaws among the ruins of Verulamium. A later king, possibly Canute, gave permission to demolish the buildings except one tower, which was to be left standing as a token of royal ownership, and there it remained, a lasting irritation to the Abbey, until Saxon rule had gone and Norman kings were in power. It was King Stephen who visited the Abbot, and as he was somewhat hard-up, he allowed the final demolition in return for a cash hand-out.

The Saxon monastery retained its aristocratic flavour. One or possibly two of the earliest Abbots were of royal blood, and two others were sons of earls, while an early Norman monk was Robert, Earl of Northumberland, who gave the Abbey the site of Tynemouth Priory, and this became an important and useful daughter-house. There was nothing democratic about St Albans Abbey, no befriending clever sons of villeins and educating them to take a place in the royal civil service, as often happened in other Houses. One of the most brilliant Abbots was looked down on by his monks because he was *only* the son of a merchant. The monks as a whole were snobs.

During the rule of the fourth Saxon Abbot, a curious incident is said to have occurred. Some Danes broke open the shrine of the saint and carried off his bones to Denmark, where they enshrined them in a church in Odense, still dedicated to St Alban. The Danes used to claim that they still held the bones, and told a visiting party from St Albans City Council so, but the tomb once claimed for St Alban is now ascribed to the brother of Canute.

The Abbey did not take this theft kindly, and the Sacristan and another monk went over to Denmark and joined the Danish church making plans, aiming to recover the relics. They eventually succeeded, and returned to St Albans in triumph, but the Danes declared that they knew what was going on and had retained the bones, palming off false relics on the Englishmen. It was not until 1966 that they tacitly admitted the true story! Matthew Paris told it centuries ago, after he had himself heard it from some St Albans diplomats who had taken royal service in Denmark, and then returned home to their own king.

There is an amusing sequel to the tale. It is told of Abbot Leofric II that, hearing a rumour in the late tenth century that there was to be another raid by the Danes, he feared for the safety of the bones and requested asylum for them at Ely. But he had doubts of the honesty of the Ely monks, and he sent anonymous bones to Ely and hid the authentic bones in a hole in the Abbey wall. The Danes did not come so the Abbot requested the return of the bones. They were duly returned, but the doubts of Abbot Leofric were justified, and he had to tell the Ely monks that they were found out, as he had prudently marked the ones he sent. He also announced that they had never had the real bones, which he reinstated in their place at St Albans. The monks of Ely were shameless, and declared that they proposed to keep the bones of our saint. The Abbot of St Albans went to law on the matter and started one of the most famous lawsuits of all time, which lasted for a century, until in Norman times, Pope Adrian IV made the monks of Ely own up, and there was once again only one St Alban in England.

The coming of the Normans brought changes to St Albans as elsewhere, the chief of these affecting the Abbey. The Conqueror had no love for the Abbey, though we do not know why. It is said that Fritheric, the last Saxon Abbot, went to William at Berkhamsted and demanded that he should swear on the bones of Alban (which he had taken with him) that he should observe the ancient laws of England. If the story is true, Fritheric must have been either a brave man or a lunatic. In face of the devastating rage of William, he fled to Ely for safety, and stayed there till he died. The bones had had yet another adventure. William was prepared to vent his anger on the Abbey itself and close it down, but fortunately his new Archbishop of Canterbury, Lanfranc, wanted it for his godson, Paul de Caen, and persuaded William to spare it. Paul became the first Norman Abbot. The town was then quite small. Domesday Book lists forty-six burgesses, thirteen cottagers, four Frenchmen, and sixteen serfs. The total population must have been about four hundred and sixty. The income was eleven pounds fourteen shillings yearly with the rents of three mills worth forty shillings yearly. The woodland where seven thousand pigs roamed was worth forty shillings more. The whole rents due amounted to twenty pounds, having appreciated in value by eight pounds since the reign of Edward the Confessor. A deer park and a fishpond are also mentioned.

Paul de Caen demolished the Saxon Abbey, waxing scornful about the condition of the existing buildings, and described his predecessors somewhat discourteously as '*rudes et idiotas*'. The new building was not re-consecrated until 1116. It cost much less than might have been expected, for a late Saxon Abbot had wanted to do the same and had collected masses of Roman bricks, which he obtained by organising a major demolition of the remains of Verulamium. When Paul started building, there were stacks of building materials waiting to be used. The only bits of the Saxon Abbey considered worthy of re-use were some balusters, which can be seen set in the triforium of the transepts. Henry I did not share the Conqueror's dislike of the Abbey, and he attended the re-dedication with his Queen, and his son, the future ill-fated victim of the wreck of the White Ship. They were accompanied by a brilliant concourse of English and foreign notabilities. The Abbot became a great noble, and his House acquired such a high reputation that before long applications for admission to the ranks of the monks were so many that numbers had to be limited to a hundred. At the Council of Tours, the Abbot of St Albans took precedence over all the English Abbots present.

Following the example of the Pope, Henry II gave St Albans Abbey a grant of liberties which gave it 'all liberties which kingly power can confer on any church'. Henry II's son, John, was perhaps the most unpopular king who ever reigned over this country, and he succeeded in alienating all classes of the community. By 1213 discontent was acute, and the Archbishop of Canterbury led the discontented. The King realised the danger and gave way to the extent of summoning a Great Council, to assemble at St Albans to hear the Justiciar state to what redress the King would agree. At this assembly the Archbishop produced a charter of Henry I which spoke of the liberties of freemen. This was discussed and amendments suggested, and the modified document was submitted to another meeting at St Paul's a few months later. After a third great meeting of tenants in chief at Bury St Edmunds, the document appeared in its final form at Runnymede, as Magna Carta. This document has often been called the beginning of the rule of law, a landmark in the history of the whole democratic world, but it has a special significance for St Albans, for to that Great Council came, not only the great men of Church and State, but knights of the shire, and the reeve and four freemen of every township on the royal estates. It was the beginning of Parliament, and inevitably, though later, the beginning of the House of Commons. St Albans saw its birth, and her citizens watched with pride, as in June 1968, one of the 13th century copies of Magna Carta was carried through our streets in procession to the Abbey, where it was guarded by four soldiers during a commemorative service.

As the years passed, the monks largely ceased to perform the essential rule laid down by St Benedict. They did not obey the order that they should do physical work—'To labour is to pray' said their founder—but by the 13th century, they passed over the humble daily tasks to lay-brothers and servants, farm-workers, cooks, and other domestics, retaining themselves the more intellectual and professional tasks. The monks were doctors, architects, workers in precious metals, and producers of books with exquisite illuminations, sometimes employing temporary assistants for special work. For example, the talented artists who painted the murals in the nave, were not all monks of the Abbey; one of the family of goldsmiths nicknamed 'the incomparable goldsmith' was the nephew of one of the monks and had done work at other monasteries.

The Abbey was not a mild owner and landlord to the inhabitants who were under its jurisdiction. Its manorial tenants paid all the dues which were customary, but whereas on other manors, the heriot payable on the death of the tenant was usually the best beast on the holding, St Albans Abbey demanded all the furniture as well.

From the early 14th century, though the grandeur of the life led by the Abbots, and the pride of the monastic community grew, their financial position was not that good, and the Abbey was often on the brink of bankruptcy. Though it had great possessions and apparent wealth, those possessions belonged, not to the community, but to the Saint, and could not (or at least, should not) be sold or otherwise disposed of. Some Abbots were extravagant, like Abbot Hugh of Eversden, friend of Edward II. His finances were so bad that he had to maintain a guard at the gate to keep out the bailiffs, yet began to build the beautiful Lady Chapel, and at the same time, had to face the costly repair due to the crash in 1323 when several of the great Norman pillars fell, bringing down the roof of the south aisle. Similarly, a few years before the Peasants' Revolt, the main gateway was destroyed in a storm which lasted five days and blew down the spire of Norwich Cathedral.

Against this may be set the periods of rule of some of our greatest Abbots: Richard of Wallingford, Michael of Mentmore, and Thomas de la Mare. Richard was a brilliant mathematician, who put his mathematics to use as a practical financier, reforming the solvency of the Abbey. Unfortunately, he died after nine years, leaving as legacy an astronomical clock, still going 200 years later. He was succeeded by Mentmore, who successfully restored discipline, though his thirteen years' rule was broken by the outbreak of the Black Death; over three quarters of the community died. Perhaps the greatest of all the Abbots was Thomas de la Mare, whose brother was Speaker of the House of Commons. He was outstanding as a financier, he earned the affection and respect of his monks, though not the affection of the town. He was honoured by his friendship with the Black Prince, who, when he held King John of France prisoner after the Battle of Poitiers, sent him to St Albans to the custody of his friend. For a short time, the French monarch stayed in a private house in French Row, a house which later became an inn, named the Fleur de Lys. The public house which replaced it, though largely rebuilt, still retains some traces of the fourteenth century. He ruled for nearly fifty years, dying just before the beginning of the fifteenth century. After his time, relations between Abbey and town deteriorated, the town becoming so disaffected that it became a hotbed of Lollardy. The showers of Lollard leaflets which were strewn in the streets on one occasion offer proof of the advance of education among the inhabitants. Early in the 15th century, the townsfolk built the Clock Tower, a municipal property, unlike any other town clock tower in the country. The only similar one was built to act as a guard-tower from incursions from the Border raiders, but St Albans Clock Tower was entirely peaceful, and held a curfew bell.

By the early 16th century, the last traces of the Abbey's glory were steadily vanishing, along with the Middle Ages. St Albans was approaching modern times, and though some building, such as the lovely High Altar Screen was still undertaken, and the Ramryge chantry followed the new development of fan-vaulting, no more additions were to be made to the beauties of the structure. The Abbot still lived like a great noble, dining with visitors in the refectory with what now seems like ridiculous pomp. Robert Shrimpton, who saw the great changes which befell the Abbey told of the wonder-working image of the saint, and of the ludicrous doings on the days when the image was carried round the town. The bearers put it down outside the Clock Tower and then pretended that it could not be lifted, until the Abbot came and ordered 'St Alban, come home' and the saint meekly obeyed.

Shrimpton lived to be about a hundred years of age, becom ng three times Mayor of St Albans, outliving Elizabeth by over two years.

Some of the property of the Abbey had already been alienated before the final dissolution took place. There had been two leper hospitals founded in the early Middle Ages, one for men, St Julians, the other for women, St Mary de Pratis, or the Pré. There seem to have been no women lepers, and the Pré functioned as a small religious house. When on the death of the Abbot, Cardinal Wolsey was given the abbacy (a deliberate slight on the dignity of the Abbey), he welcomed the chance of suppressing some of the smaller cells, such as the Pré, and diverted their assets to his newly proposed foundation at Oxford. The nuns at Pré, reduced to five by the death of the Prioress, closed up and left of their own volition, and Wolsey let the property on thirty years' lease. After the fall of Wolsey, Robert Catton was appointed Abbot—the only Abbot of St Albans to be sacked, which he richly deserved. The last Abbot was Richard Boreman, who valiantly struggled to keep the organisation going, was sent to prison for failing to pay the due taxes, scraped up enough money to pay them once more and then gave up and surrendered the Abbey and all its possessions to the king's hand, he and his monks leaving the building and retiring on pensions to private life. The aristocratic social standing of the community prevented the monks suffering, as in many other monasteries, and there is no record of any protests being made, though there must have been cases of private heartbreak. The ex-Abbot continued to take an interest in local matters, and hoped that the Abbey would be revived under Mary Tudor, until her death.

The monastic land, with the land around was granted to Sir Richard Lee, a military engineer, and a friend of Henry VIII. Lee sold the site of the monastery buildings to Boreman, who presented it to Mary Tudor. Consequently, it came back into Royal hands. Lee retained Sopwell and its lands, which he altered and from which he formed a country house to supplement his town house, The Mansion in St Peter's Street. Much of the conventual premises was pulled down and a great deal of new building put up with the quantity of cheap building material which came onto the market.

The largest acquisition of Abbey property was made by Ralph Rowlatt, who obtained Gorhambury, the Pré, the manor of Westwick, the manor of Sandridge, the manor of Napsbury, a house on Holywell Hill, a number of manors in Hertfordshire outside St Albans and a number of church advowsons. One of his descendants was Sarah Jennings, who became the Duchess of Marlborough.

Building the Abbey. (Permission of British Lib. Cott. MS Nero. D1.)

ABOVE: Saxon Balusters in South Transept.

LEFT: Norman doorway to Slype.

RIGHT: North Transept; Norman piers of Crossing.

LEFT: Early English Arches, in retro-choir.

RIGHT: Norman Tower, built of Roman bricks.

BELOW: Pointed oval Seal of Abbey, 12th cent.; Alban seated on carved throne.

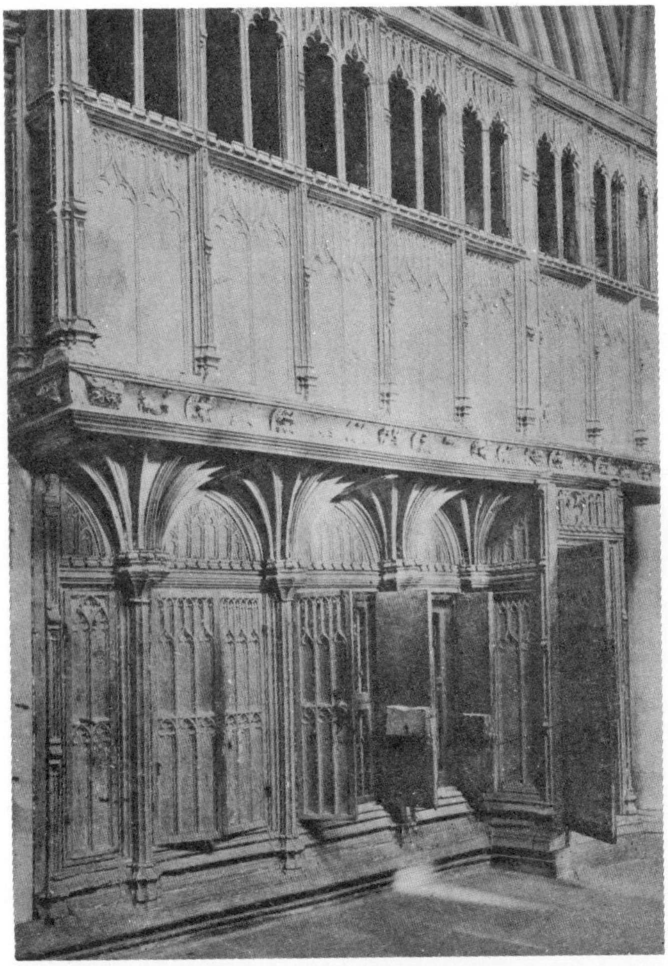 

LEFT: The Watching Gallery.

RIGHT: Rear of Watching Gallery.

BELOW: Carvings on Watching Gallery.

ABOVE LEFT: Staircase to Watching Gallery, and

RIGHT: High Altar Screen.

BELOW LEFT: Abbot's Door and RIGHT: Carved heads; Triforium in Nave.

LEFT : Mural in the North Transept; D

CENTRE LEFT : Old West I

CENTRE RIGHT : Lady Cha

RIGHT : Humphrey, Duke of Gloucest
being received into the Fraternity of St A
(British Library)

BELOW LEFT : Chantry tomb of Humphrey

BELOW RIGHT : Great Gate of Abbey. Now p

omas.

wife
y, 1431.

loucester.

bans School.

Brass of Abbot Thomas de la Mare.

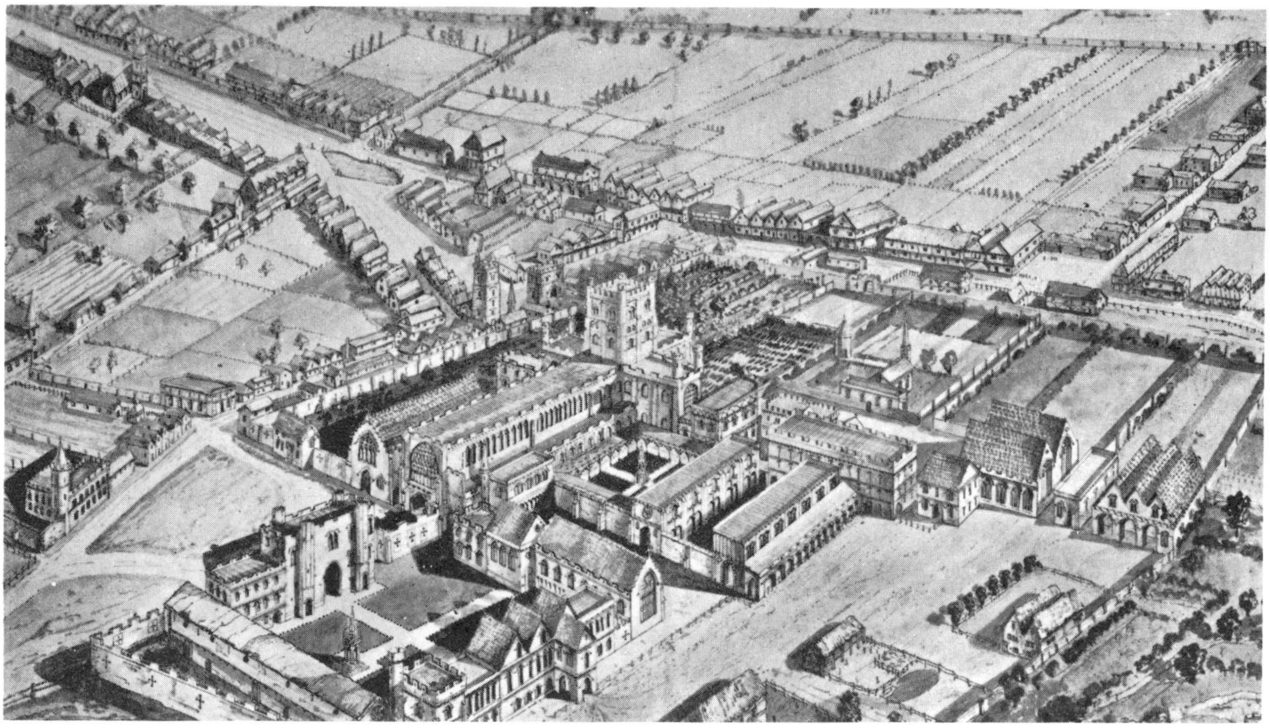

ABOVE: Reconstruction of the Abbey in its great day, before the Dissolution.

BELOW: Remains of the Great Guesthouse, in the 18th cent.

ABOVE: Unrestored Abbey, 1737.

BELOW: Old West End of Abbey, 1805.

Mitre and Plainsong

After the Dissolution, the domestic buildings of the monastery were largely demolished, though the stables remained in the occupation of a local farmer until the 18th century. Two of the gates were kept in use—the Great Gate and the Waxhouse gate, the passage of both still in use; the gate giving access to the Sumpter Yard had a house above it, which survived until it was pulled down in the 19th century. The back of a fireplace can still be seen jutting into the roadway of the Sumpter Yard. The School was restarted in the Lady Chapel and the main building became a parish church, which soon began to show rough handling. The Shrine disappeared; its pedestal, broken into fragments, was used to fill in the early English arches between the Saint's Chapel and the retro-choir to the east. That was turned into a passage, with entrances at north and south giving access to the School. All the Saints' statues were destroyed, but the High Altar remained, with empty spaces like blind eyes in its fabric. The mural paintings were whitewashed over, and the building soon showed signs of neglect. In his Will, Sir Ralph Rowlatt asked to be buried 'Yf it chance to be a place convenient for burial in our lady chapel within the late monastery of St Alban where my wyfe lyeth and my sonne. And yf the same shal be noo such place mete for burial then I will my body to be buried within the chapel of St Andrew,' which looks as if the Abbey was already neglected only three years after the Dissolution. True or not, it was openly described as 'decayed' in the early seventeenth century. By the early nineteenth century the holes in the roof were so bad that Divine Service could not be celebrated. In the first half of the nineteenth century, attempts were made to raise funds, and in 1856 Sir Gilbert Scott was commissioned to carry out repair-work, but none of these efforts was sufficient to pay for an adequate restoration. For some time a committee continued these efforts, and a certain amount of work was done, but the committee added a famous lawyer to their number. He wanted them to carry out a far-reaching restoration, to which they agreed. They were led on by Sir Edmund Beckett, or Lord Grimthorpe as he later became, to more and more ambitious schemes, until they realised that they must submit to all his demands. He obtained a Faculty, which to all intents and purposes put the Abbey into his hands. His work involved the destruction of much of the fabric which could and should have been preserved, but no one ventured to combat his obstinacy and overbearing temper, or risk the loss of his powerful purse. He is said to have spent about half a million pounds, a colossal sum in the 1870s. But to do him justice, though he was not the great architectural authority he believed, had he not done what he did, we should have no Abbey to-day. He might have done worse. The well known architects of the time were capable of anything, even, in some places, completely destroying ancient churches and building Victorian Gothic imitations in their place. His head and winged shoulders appear in the west porch. In 1877 the Abbey was raised to the status of a Cathedral, and the Bishop of Rochester was named its first Bishop, but the restorations were still incomplete and Bishop Claughton could not be formally enthroned until 1879. The Rector became the Dean in 1900.

The three mediaeval churches, St Michael's, St Peter's and St Stephen's take pride of place after the Abbey. They are all reputed to have been founded by Abbot Ulsinus in AD 948, and a pageant was performed in their honour in 1948. As with many buildings of Saxon foundation the dates are dubious, but there can be little discrepancy with tradition in St Michael's, since it has obviously Saxon arches as main features, with remains of later work. It may be as old as the Abbey, since it is built within the area of the Roman Forum, and possibly on the site of the basilica. The earliest church consisted of a nave and chancel only. The pre-Conquest windows were enlarged, probably in the early 11th century, and were discovered when Sir Gilbert Scott restored the church in 1866. In the Grimthorpe era, the tower was transferred to the West end, thus altering the ancient plan.

After the Dissolution, it became the church of the owners of Gorhambury—the Bacons and Grimstons. Francis Bacon wanted to be buried there, but the spite of his estranged wife prevented this, and his grave is unknown, but his kinsman, Sir Thomas Meautys, put a striking seated figure of Bacon as a memorial in the chancel of the church. The Bacons were strong Puritans, and the chaplain of Gorhambury became the Vicar of the church, though he was not allowed to continue, in spite of continued efforts by Lady Bacon to reinstate him.

St Peter's and St Stephen's do not show their age as clearly as St Michael's, though both have plenty of proofs of their antiquity, but the appearance of St Peter's was drastically altered by Grimthorpe. Each contains some feature from an earlier day. St. Stephen's has Norman work, and a relic of the Scottish wars in the shape of a fine lectern, taken from Holyroodhouse and brought back to St Albans. St Peter's contains a later relic—the portrait of a famous parishioner. This was Edward Strong, master-mason to Wren during the building of St Paul's Cathedral after the Great Fire. Stone built himself a house opposite the church in St Peter's Street, which still stands and is used as offices.

There are a number of other buildings of the Established Church, such as St Paul's in Hatfield Road, and a building which takes one to Italy—Christ Church in Verulam Road, originally designed as a Roman Catholic place of worship. Before it was finished, the Catholics gave up the project, for lack of funds. A local lady, Mrs Worley, took the building over and paid for its completion as an Anglican Church. It remained independent of the Church authorities, appointing its own parson, paying his salary and maintaining the fabric. It remained under this unusual arrangement for some years before it submitted to orthodox Anglican authority. Membership declined with the growth of new housing estates, and the building was sold in 1975, put to other uses, and a new Church, St Andrew's, founded in the New Green's area as a daughter of Christ Church, absorbed the congregation. Another new church, St Julian's, daughter to St Stephen's was founded in the first half of the twentieth century on another housing estate.

The two remaining Anglican churches are St Saviour's in Sandpit Lane and St Mary's on the Marshalswick development. Such is St Albans' ecumenical spirit today that while Marshalswick Baptist Church was in the building, the Baptist congregation enjoyed the hospitality of St Mary's, who lent their schoolroom for Baptist services.

As there had been Lollards in pre-Reformation St Albans, so there were Puritans in Tudor times. In Mary's reign there were no local martyrs, but one Protestant was burnt at the stake in Romeland. George Tankerfield was a Barnet baker. His death was a warning to the townspeople, who had shown no great grief at the passing of their monastic masters. His death was an isolated event, but as soon as Elizabeth gained the throne, and England became Protestant, groups of people gathered to whom Elizabethan Protestantism was not sufficiently advanced. Among the most prominent Puritans were the Bacons and the Pembertons. Laud's attempts to enforce conformity met with much quiet resistance. When Dr Prynne, who wrote against stage plays, and had one ear cropped, was sent to have the other ear cropped, he was brought through St Albans. A crowd gathered and lustily cheered him, which was not the effect desired by the authorities. There was at least one well-known Baptist in the town as early as 1646, and by tradition Dagnall Street Baptist Church has dated its foundation to the year 1640, though it had no meeting-house then, but was attached to the community at Kensworth. While it was still illegal to be a Baptist, the St Albans sect would tramp the twelve miles to Kensworth and back every Sunday. The names of these people survive in a contemporary manuscript volume. An early meetinghouse in Dagnall Street was superceded in 1720 by the first church on its present site. In 1859, important alterations were made and one of the only five organs in the town was erected in the building. No further changes were made until the present church was built in 1885. It possesses two treasures. One is a chair said to have belonged to the Baptist Elizabethan Mayor, who presented a speech of welcome to the Queen on one of her visits to the town, probably on her way to Gorhambury. This chair is placed before a table, believed to originally belong to John Bunyan. It serves as a Communion table. Bunyan had friends in the neighbourhood. There was at one time a cottage, known as Bunyan's Cottage, near Sandridge, but nothing survives but one chimney.

At the Restoration, many of the nonconformist clergy, who had replaced conforming clergy, were turned out. One of these, who had been installed at the Abbey, was a distinguished divine named Nathaniel Partridge.

Nonconformity went underground until the Toleration Act was passed in the next reign. By the late 18th century, for some reason, new premises were needed; the sect found them in the Cotton Mill. An Independent Chapel was built in Lower Dagnall Street which became one of the earliest Unitarian Chapels in England. While it was Independent it provided religious solace to two remarkable men. Philip Doddridge had been a pupil at a school for nonconformists, housed in Newland Squillers House, where Alban Coxe had lived. Dr Doddridge became a hymn writer and left us the much-loved words of 'O God of Bethel'. The other distinguished Dissenter was a doctor, who kept a 'College for the Insane' (hence College Street), where he cared for the mentally sick with a remarkably modern flavour. Poet William Cowper was his patient more than once, and they attended the Independent Chapel together. In 1811, a new Independent, afterwards Congregational Chapel was built.

Mid-19th century there was a small Roman Catholic congregation in the town. After their original financial failure with Christ Church, some years later they made another and more successful attempt, but they were still dogged by frustration, when a disastrous fire struck their London Road church. From the shell a garage eventually emerged. They succeeded at the third attempt, and dedicated their church to Saints Alban and Stephen.

In Homewood Road, the Presbyterian Church has joined with Trinity Church to form a United Reformed Church, and there is an active body of the Salvation Army, with a main Citadel in the centre of the city, and a branch in Camp Road. The 'War Cry' is printed in St Albans and the instruments for their fine Bands are made here too.

There are a number of charities dating from the sixteenth to twentieth centuries. Many involve quite small sums and many are distributed by the Mayor. Some are in the disposal of one or other of the churches. There are several foundations of almshouses, and the earliest to still survive is the Raynshaw Charity in Spicer Street. Richard Raynshaw was a retired Yeoman of the Guard, who obtained a thirty years' lease of the premises of the Hospital of St Mary de Pratis, or the Pré from Cardinal Wolsey, who was briefly Abbot. Wolsey had taken possession of The Pré following the death of the prioress, when the remaining five or six nuns closed up and left the buildings untenanted. After the Dissolution Raynshaw obtained a lease from Ralph Rowlatt, who became the owner of the Gorhambury estates. By his will, Raynshaw left property to some citizens of St Albans, which on their death, was to revert to the corporation of St Albans to found almshouses, funds to be found in the rent of adjoining property which became an inn, the Vine. This charity is still in existence, though the almshouses have been rebuilt, and are managed by a committee.

Another foundation of almshouses still in existence is The Marlborough Almshouses, founded by Sarah, widow of John Churchill the famous soldier. Sarah was the daughter of John Jennings of Sandridge and Holywell house. She was possibly born at Water End but was christened in the Abbey, and when she married, she received Holywell House as part of her dowry. Churchill was far from wealthy, so the couple made their home in St Albans and the Tudor building underwent considerable alteration. The Marlboroughs used the house as a favourite dwelling, raised their family, and entertained Royalty there. Even after the Palace of Blenheim was built for them, Sarah said that she liked it better than any house she had seen. After the death of Marlborough, she purchased the Manor House of Newland Squillers, near the top of Cock Lane, now Hatfield Road, pulled it down and built the present almshouses, round three sides of a square garden. The buildings are maintained by a committee, and have been recently brought up to date, with flats upstairs for single or widowed tenants, and married couples on the ground floor. Each flat has a garden, but the central lawn and flower-beds in the quadrangle are maintained by the Parks Department. Until a few years ago, the centre of the lawn was occupied by a large cedar tree, perhaps planted by Sarah herself.

There is another pleasant block of almshouses opposite St Peter's Church—the Pemberton Almshouses, which were administered by St Peter's Church authorities, until after the Second World War the Church could no longer afford their upkeep. Roger Pemberton was out shooting with his bow, and accidentally shot and killed a poor widow. He built the almshouses in expiation. The building now belongs to the City Council which lets it as old folks' accommodation.

There are other bequests of living accommodation in the city, and one or two instances of benefits being transferred to modern houses to replace charities shifted for road-widening in the centre of the town, such as the William Powell, which used to be two cottages in Victoria Street, and is now two houses in Dickens Close. Others have been remodelled, such as the May Clarke flatlets in Catherine Street. This benefice was originally held by some cottages which faced up St Peter's Street, on the site of the front of the Town Hall, and was transferred to Catherine Street when the Town Hall was built about 1829.

In the South Transept of the Abbey there can be seen three old dole cupboards. These house the Skelton Bread Dole, founded in 1628, which provides newly baked loaves to be given to poor women of the Abbey every Sunday morning. The loaves are very small!

In addition to these charities there are a large number of gifts of small sums of money, clothing, coal and blankets. Many of these are in the gift of one or other of the churches; others of them were left to the town for the benefit of its poor, and these are distributed by the Mayor.

The Abbey today.

ABOVE LEFT: Abbey, East End, and RIGHT:
Easter Pilgrimage of Youth.

BELOW LEFT: The Bishop, Rt Rev Robert Runcie and
RIGHT: The Dean, Very Rev Peter Moore.

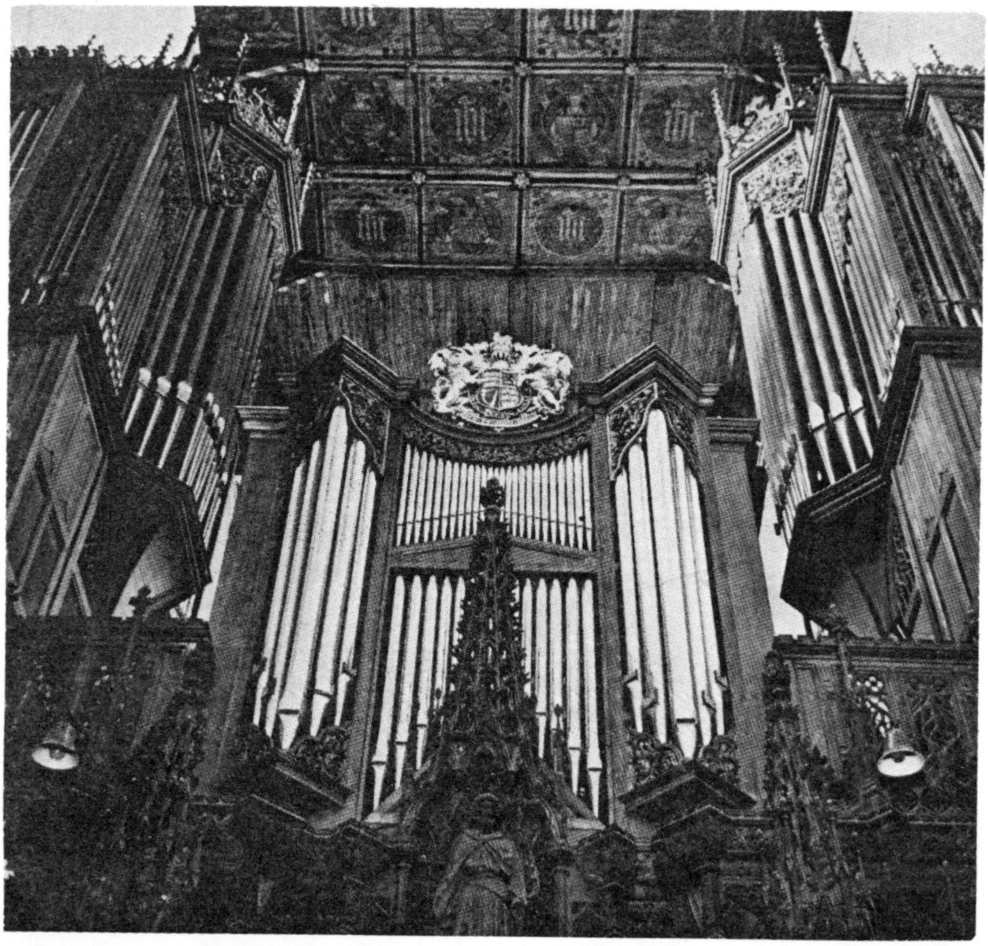

ABOVE: The Great Organ.

BELOW: The Abbey, as it stands high above the city. (Kitton)

ABOVE LEFT: Bust of Lord Grimthorpe in West Porch of Abbey, showing him as St Matthew.

RIGHT: St Michael's Church, 1834.

BELOW: St Michael's today.

BELOW RIGHT: Statue of Francis Bacon in St Michael's.

LEFT: Jacobean pulpit in St Michael's Church.

ABOVE: St Peter's Church about 1862, before restoration.

BELOW: St Peter's today with Green and War Memorial. (Founded about 948)

LEFT: St Stephen's Church. (Founded about 948)

RIGHT: Christ Church, now closed.

BELOW: St Saviour's Church.

LEFT: Dagnall Street Baptist Church and BELOW: Inside the Church.

INSET: Rev W. J. A. Turner, BA, pastor of Dagnall Street Church.

RIGHT: Trinity Reformed Church.

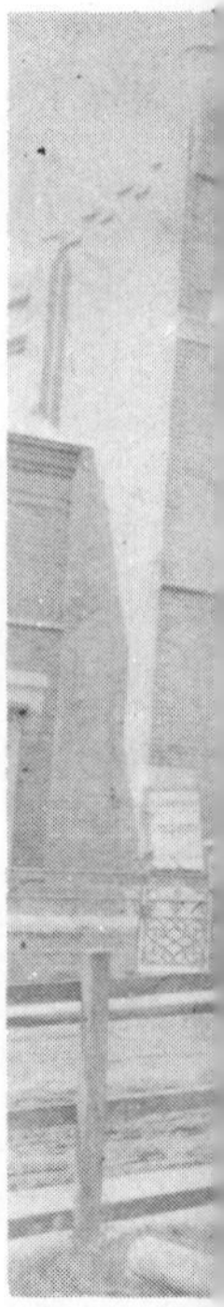

ABOVE LEFT TO RIG
The Independent Ch
Church, now close
Cl

LEFT CENTRE: Pe
M

CENTRE: The Vin
for upkeep of

BELOW R

ɔorough Road Methodist Church;
ɜr Street; The Tabernacle Baptist
ɲn Army Citadel; and Bunyan's
ɔleman Green.

ɩlmshouses, and BELOW LEFT:
h Almshouses.

of funds assigned by Raynshaw.
ɩuses, now a private house.

ɩe cupboard in Abbey.

ABOVE: Plaque on site of Castle Inn, on the corner of Shropshire Lane, now Victoria Street.

BELOW: Hall Place, where Henry VI rested at time of First Battle of St Albans, 1455.

Men at Arms

Except for two periods, one in the early 13th century, the other in the second half of the 15th, St Albans was spared the ravages of war throughout the rule of the monastery; Mother Church and her religious communities were generally peaceful. In the earliest of these periods, King John's misrule brought the Dauphin's French army to St Albans. They committed serious excesses, threatened the Abbey, were quartered in the street alongside the Market place, and left their name for all time to 'French Row'. With the death of John, large numbers of his opponents left the Dauphin, and supported the child-king, Henry III. This volte-face made little difference to the inhabitants of St Albans, for the followers of Faulkes de Breaute were just as devastating as the Frenchmen.

St Albans was drawn into contact with the Hundred Years' War. The Black Prince was a personal friend of the Abbot, who received the King of France as a prisoner after Poitiers. The town escaped upheavals for another century, save for the rising of the peasants in 1381. Little disturbance arose from their activities. Mainly highly respectable businessmen, they largely succeeded in restraining the mild excesses of their followers against the Abbey, which involved some destruction of fences, some burning of documents, and one raid on the Abbey Gateway, not much to do with peasants.

But St Albans saw real armies in 1455, during the Wars of the Roses. The first battle in 1455, was won by the Yorkists, the Duke of Somerset dying on the steps of the Castle Inn, on the corner of Shropshire Lane (now Victoria Street). The King was slightly wounded, and was taken to the home of a county official, Edmund Westby, whose house, Hall Place, stood until 1917.

Six years later the two armies clashed again in the city. This time the Yorkists were in command of the town, their army in the St Peter's Street area. The Lancastrians had been fighting in the Midlands, and came along Watling Street, led by Queen Margaret. They reached the top of George Street, but the Yorkists massed in the vicinity of the Clock Tower, and blocked their way. Against such strong resistance, Margaret drew her army back down George and Fishpool Streets, turned right at Gonnerston near St Michael's Bridge, and travelled along a lane parallel to the modern Branch Road to Folly Lane (then Claypits Lane). This lane led, as it still does, directly into the town by Catherine Lane (now Street) to one of the defensive gates. The Catherine Bars were not strongly defended, a fatal error on the part of the Yorkist commander, and Margaret's forces broke through into the northern end of St Peter's Street, between the two parts of the Yorkist army. She defeated them south of St Peter's Church, and then faced the other way, attacked the Yorkists in the Bowgate, driving them on to Barnet Heath (now Bernard's Heath). Again she won, and drove the battered remnants to Nomansland Common, whence the demoralised Yorkists fled in all directions. Margaret led her triumphant army into St Albans, and there ensued a terrifying time for the town, as the Lancastrian troops were let loose on the unfortunate citizens with Margaret's permission to loot as they would. The Yorkists had also looted, but they were not as undisciplined as their adversaries. Even the Queen herself joined in, and the chronicle says bitterly that she took with her the Abbey's best jewel. Successive Abbots had sat on the fence, and suffered at the hands of both sides, but the destruction now was greater at the hands of the Red Rose, and too late, the Abbot came down for the Yorkist cause. The final victor was Henry VII, and there was no one then to protect the Abbey from its enemy, Cardinal Morton. He accused the Abbot of grave irregularities of conduct, though history has failed to show that the charges were valid.

Henceforth, the town saw no more armies until the Tudors had come and gone, and the only connexion with war was when the Spaniards attempted to invade. As the Armada threatened our shores, the trainbands of Hertfordshire were given the honour of providing the guard for Elizabeth when she reviewed her soldiers at Tilbury. On this historic occasion, an entry was made in the Minutes of the Council: 'After this Court there was levied of the inhabitants of this Borough for conduct money for 52 soldiers of this Borough, after the rate of 6s 8d for every soldier, and for the conveyance of their armour to Tillburie and to conduct them to their Captain. Sum total . . . 19 8 6.' The whole amount was distributed as follows:— 'Paid to Francis Stepney, Sir John Brockett's Clerk, for conduct money for 52 men at 6s 8d for every man 17 6 8. To Richard Weldon for his cart to carry their arms to Tillburie 1 10 0. The charge of those who conveyed the soldiers and their armour from St Albans to Barnet to their Captain . . . 0 ii 6. Total . . . 19 8 2. Now in Mr Mayor's hands only 0 0 4.

'After this Court the soldiers and their armour being at the Camp at Tillburie, a warrant was directed to the High Constables to levy £20 or thereabouts to pay for certain carts detained at the camp to attend upon 300 soldiers which went from this part, to carry and re-carry necessaries for them, which was at the rate of £3 6s 8d for every half hundred of the soldiers and because there went out of this town half a hundred and better therefore there was levied of the inhabitants of this town and sent to the Captain of the Camp £3 11s and 20d Mr Mayor laid out; for the whole war £3 12s 8d.' Was ever war waged so cheaply before?

Thenceforth, St Albans seems to have enjoyed tranquillity for some long time. Not until the Civil War were soldiers seen in St Albans again. The power of the Abbey had gone, and only the townsfolk exercised influence, within their own boundaries. The new men of power were the middle class, who lived not in great houses, but like the Jenningses in Holywell Hill, and the Pembertons in St Peter's Street—a natural reaction from the oppressive authority of the Abbots. For many years the town had been rebellious, and once the monastic grip had gone, they took to running their own affairs and resented taking orders from elsewhere. Understandably they were for Parliament and against the King, especially when their pockets were touched. The first opposition came over ship money. In 1640 the townsfolk sent a petition accusing the High Sheriff of over-rigorous levying of that tax. One of the St Albans MPs was Sir John Jennings of Sandridge and Holywell House, and he was succeeded in the Long Parliament by his son. Such men truly represented their constituents. At the beginning of the struggle there was less opposition to the Monarchy as such, but more to the use Charles made of it.

The Long Parliament had hardly met before petitions began to come in and the very first was presented by a Hertfordshire man, Arthur, afterwards Lord Capel, supported by a Member, afterwards to take up residence in St Albans, Sir Harbottle Grimston. The authorities received proclamations from both sides, and found themselves faced with the question of which to proclaim. In 1641, William New was Mayor of St Albans; he chose wrongly and read a proclamation issued by the King. He was forthwith summoned before the Bar of the House of Commons to make his excuses, and these not proving satisfactory, he was committed to the Fleet prison. When he was released, he considered that the expenses of his stay were reasonable Mayoral expenses and charged them up to the Council, but that body soon taught him better.

By this time war was clearly imminent, and both sides were arming and training. Some people were departing from London into the countryside. For example, Lady Sussex had rented Gorhambury from Sir Thomas Meautys for herself and her 'good old man' as she called him. As war loomed she became more and more worried. She wrote to Sir Harry Verney 'These distracted times put us all in great disorders but I hope that we shall not be killed yet.' In 1642, when war was actually starting, St Albans became the headquarters of the army of the Earl of Essex, and her fears increased, so she wrote to him begging for protection for Gorhambury, and the earl signed an order of protection on November 4th 1642. Five days later she wrote to Verney that she had sent a chest of plate to a goldsmith and that she was barricading her doors or as many as she could. A week or so later, she wrote that she was putting her hangings and best stuff in one of the round turrets over her chamber and walling them up. She certainly took liberties with rented property.

St Albans had become a centre for recruiting the parliamentary army. One of the local gentlemen was Col Alban Coxc of the manor house of Newland Squillers, which occupied the site of the later Marlborough Almshouses. He was a personal friend of Oliver Cromwell, who stayed with him on occasion. Coxe undertook the training of the cavalry force raised in the town, which became part of the army of the Earl of Essex, about two thousand men who arrived in St Albans in August 1642. The army was poorly disciplined and the pillory in St Albans was rendered portable so that it could be set up in the parts of the town where the army was billeted.

The gentry of St Albans joined with other Eastern Counties to set up a Parliamentary Council of War. This included Sir John Garrard of Wheathampstead, Richard Jennings, Henry Meautys, John and Ralph Pemberton, Sir John Wittewrong of Rothamstead, John Rowbotham, the owner of Newland Squillers, and the Mayor of St Albans. Then the King appointed Thomas Coningsby to be High Sheriff, an unfortunate choice. In January 1643 he arrived from South Mimms with a strong following to take advantage of a Market Day audience, and read a Royal proclamation, calling on the militia to resist anyone forming a force in favour of Parliament and calling on all citizens to arrest such people. He read the document from the steps of the Eleanor Cross. Suddenly, from the junction of Holywell Hill and High Street, there was a stir and round the corner rode Cromwell with twenty troopers, who charged the Sheriff's party, which withdrew and fought in the yard of the Red Lion. Coningsby was captured and sent to London as a prisoner. He got off lightly in comparison with a mediaeval High Sheriff, who rode into St Albans to make an unpopular proclamation and who was lynched by the indignant citizens. Lady Sussex wrote, 'I hope in the lord pese will come . . . if there bee not i shall bee in a most miserable condisyon, for i will not stor from my goode olde lorde what some ever bee come of me.' Gorhambury remained safe from all hands but those of the lady herself, but the parish had to pay four pounds eleven shillings a week to keep eight foot-soldiers. Meanwhile the town strengthened its defences. Trenches were dug and earthworks raised, specially strong points being near St Peter's and St Stephen's Churches. In the Mayor's Accounts appear entries, 'Paid to three men for six day's work done at the townes end for mending up of the forts there at the rate of 10d a day . . . 5s.'

'For two mens work more for three days work at St Peters Street end 3s 4d.'

The weather was bad with heavy snow. All round St Albans lay a large army, hungry, discontented and mutinous for lack of pay—10,000 foot and 5,000 horse had been sanctioned by Parliament. Essex reported on December 17th that there had been a serious mutiny of several hundred men threatening to pillage the town if they were not paid. He had only a week's pay in hand, and feared loss of control. The town set up permanent stocks in the middle of the town and hoped for the best.

This tense situation lasted until the army, which now included a number of the local men, marched out. They had been reformed and reinforced with the New Model Army. After the Battle of Naseby, some of the Royalist prisoners en route to London reached St Albans. As more prisoners converged on London by other routes, there was such a 'hold-up' in the area that Col Fiennes was told to 'stay all the soldier prisoners at St Albans' till further orders. The town had to provide them with food and was glad when the bottleneck gave and they passed on. By December 1645 all danger for the area was practically over, but the war was not finished. The King, escaping from besieged Oxford, took to byways that brought him near St Albans. With his hair and beard cut off, and dressed as a servant, he reached Wheathampstead, and spent the night, probably at now-demolished Lamer Park. Although Sir John Garrard, the owner, was a commander of some of the Parliamentary forces in Hertfordshire, his personal feeling for the King must have outweighed his political allegiance, and the secret was so well kept that the King's stay is to this day a matter of conjecture.

By 1647 relations between Parliament and the Army were strained, and Cromwell, writing from Royston, threw out certain threats for the safety of London, unless the soldiers were paid. The Army moved onto St Albans, and the City of London, terror-stricken, sent a deputation to the town to meet the soldiers. The deputation made appeasing speeches, and were wined and dined by the corporation, before returning to London. A few days later, London sent a month's wages to the army with the demand that they should move to at least forty miles from the capital. On June 24th St Albans sped them on their way joyfully—St Albans is only twenty miles from London.

The King came to the town for the last time on his way to London. This was a travesty of a royal progress, with the people cheering in the streets and even the royal footmen entertained by the town.

One more incident arose from the conflict. After the surrender of Colchester, the horde of sick and hungry prisoners were sent into Hertfordshire. As this starving 'army' approached St Albans, the townsfolk took action which reflects great credit upon them. They emptied St Peter's Church of its fittings, took out the windows, as much for ventilation as to preserve the glass, and then levied a tax on themselves to provide food and medical aid. Our last direct connection with the Civil War was one of humanity and mercy.

Not again did we see fighting in our streets, except in transit to theatres of war no nearer than the Continent of Europe, until the 20th century. There is little mention of the wars of Marlborough in St Albans records, but the Council's Minute Book records that the bell-man was to have a new suit at a cost of 30s. The news of the Battle of Trafalgar came nearer home; Lord Nelson was mourned, and the news arrived by a newfangled contraption known as a semaphore set up on the top of the Clock Tower. By opening and closing the shutters, its rapidity of communication compared with the modern telephone, for it is recorded that it could send a message to Yarmouth from London and receive an answer in five minutes. It was, however, taken down in 1814, just too early for Waterloo.

Then once again the town saw war in 1914-18. St Albans met evacuees arriving disorganised, and became the headquarters of the 2nd London Division of the Territorial Army, some 20,000 troops being billeted in and around the city. King George V came to Gorhambury to review the troops on September 18th 1914, and a few days later they were again reviewed by Lord Kitchener.

In 1939 there came the Second World War, and once more there came to St Albans large numbers of people to be billeted, but evacuees, not soldiers. This time they were children from London schools, mothers and babies, pregnant women. These were official parties, under Government arrangements, but there were also men and women who sought shelter from bombing, to the number of some forty thousand. Somehow, the city managed to house them all, without losing many to enemy action from the air. Rumour suggests the first death was that of a cow on Hedge's farm. Departments of some of the London hospitals came to share St Albans institutions—The Elizabeth Garrett Anderson came to the City Hospital, and St Bartholomew's Orthopaedic section to part of Hill End. The latter remained for some time after the war ended, until part of their premises was rebuilt. Two thousand babies were born at Diocesan House by the end of 1946. Many of the evacuees found St Albans friendly and decided to stay here, and so the population grew and new houses were built. The era of housing estates appeared and drastically altered the appearance and the atmosphere of the district.

15th century archer with longbow at St Albans pageant, 1908.

ABOVE: First World War. Second London Division Territorials, at Holywell Hill.

BELOW: Women's war work, First World War—in one of the City's workrooms.

ABOVE: Review of Troops by Lord Kitchener, Gorhambury.

BELOW: Diocesan House, Maternity Hospital, 1939-45.

LEFT: Plaque at Diocesan House. Second World War.

Herts T.A. Regiment, at Abbey.

Track and Tavern

We honour Abbot Ulsinus, who according to tradition, was our first town planner. It is certainly obvious that the middle of St Albans is to this day essentially the mediaeval town whose skeleton was laid down even earlier, in Saxon days. The centre is where the Saxons put it. In the 15th century the Clock Tower was built, in the same spot as the body of the 13th century Queen Eleanor rested, before lying in state in the Abbey. From there the mediaeval streets radiated, and they still do. The new 18th century streets built by Telford—Verulam Road and London Road—met at the same point. These two roads cross a few yards away, and were reputed to carry the greatest volume of cross-road traffic in the world. The M1 has made little difference since those days, when we stood on Sunday evening on the selfsame crossroads to watch the accidents. The only other difference was the closing of the old Watling Street, at the crossing with St Stephen's Hill, which forced the line of the Roman road to turn up Holywell Hill, and then turn left into High Street. Naturally, the Clock Tower was the focal point of municipal St Albans. It was built *c* 1402-1412 and was the first municipal enterprise in the town, built and run by the citizens, not by the Abbey. Understandably the citizens clung to their rights in the Tower and committee which managed it. So determined were they to maintain control, that the committee came to include all leading citizens. At one time, not long before the Dissolution, this committee numbered eighty members, and they seem to have evolved into an unofficial borough council, closing the gap between monastic rule and the Council set up by Edward VI's Charter. Many of them feature in that first Council.

The Dissolution made the town look to other trades and industries than those of the monastic age. Quite naturally, St Albans looked to the traveller, for it had been used to travellers for hundreds of years. There were plenty of merchants and traders to occupy the beds left empty by the vanished pilgrims and the officials and hangers-on of noble visitors. So the town was dominated by the inns. The Watling Street was crowded with them, often standing side by side. The huge Bull, of which one traveller remarked that it was the largest inn he had ever seen, and where that inveterate traveller, Queen Elizabeth I is said to have stayed, has gone, but there were four or five between that and the Peahen, and more still between the Peahen and the Bell. The Chequers is still in existence, although it has changed its name to the Queen, and the Bell is still there; both have been rebuilt. In the High Street, there remains the Fleur de Lys, which has 14th century remains, and housed King John of France after Poitiers, as a prisoner in the care of Abbot Thomas de la Mare. The Fleur de Lys has recently been restored, and some of the timber-framing has been exposed. Next door is the Great Red Lion, rebuilt but still a prosperous hotel, facing one side of the Clock Tower. This narrowly missed demolition in 1700, but was fortunately saved by the objections of some of the citizens. Until the middle of the 19th century, there were some small shops built around the ground storey.

One of the oldest buildings still left is the Christopher Inn, which has some fourteenth century work, some sixteenth, some seventeenth century, and the balance of eighteenth century origin. When the City Council bought it, the owners having applied for planning permission to demolish, it was thoroughly restored, no longer as a common lodging house, but as shops and offices. On the corner of George Street and Verulam Road stands the well-restored house of a fifteenth century merchant, miscalled the Tudor Tavern, though it is considerably earlier. It is now a restaurant. George Street, with Romeland, (which is not connected with Rome, but is really Room-land) was an open space, where there was room for public meetings. Here John Ball preached, and George Tankerfield was burnt *pour encourager les autres*.

George Street is sometimes called Cook Row, largely mediaeval, and old façades mask yet older backs. Here clearance of a cellar may disclose the skeletons of a do-it-yourself burial of possible victims of a Tudor outbreak of plague, such as is sometimes casually mentioned in the contemporary minutes of the Council. Considering the fact that the greater part of the street is timber-framed it is remarkable that so much has survived. Its continuation, Fishpool Street traces its history to Saxon times, when the Royal fishpool was drained, with a small lake left to serve as stews for the monastery fish. The houses are now the subject of strict conservation. Until Telford cut Verulam Road from the Red Lion, to the north-west, to by-pass George Street and Fishpool Street, the older road had carried heavy traffic as the main route to the Midlands. More recently, with the development of Hemel Hempstead, and the excavations at Verulamium, interest in the area has increased the traffic to a degree that threatens the stability of the old buildings.

St Michael's Street is also mainly mediaeval and sixteenth century, and provides access to the Roman city. The open spaces which cover the site, and are given over to sport, add to traffic pressure.

Another road which radiates from the centre is Holywell Hill. Some visitors think it must be Hollow-way Hill, but there is still a holy well, much revered in the Middle Ages, but now covered over so that no one falls down it. In the Tudor age it was on the front lawn of what became Marlborough's house, which was just on the north bank of the River Ver and faced up the slope as far as Belmont Hill. This road had carried heavy traffic since Saxon times, when Watling Street was diverted and the vehicles forced to travel up Holywell Hill, turn left, along the High Street, and so to Fishpool Street and out of the town by Watling Street. Supplies were brought from London to the Abbey by this route, and into the Abbey Sumpter Yard, where the pack animals were unloaded. The inns in Holywell Hill were large, and some remain prosperous to this day. Several of them maintained their own coaches. The George in George Street ('The George upon the Hoop') was well-known in the fifteenth century. It was permitted to hold Mass on the premises to save pilgrims' time, and was enterprising enough in the eighteenth century to run a daily coach to London, until the railway put paid to that. When Sir Richard Lee acquired Sopwell Priory and made a country house of it, he desired to divert the alternative route from London, which passed in front of his house, too near for his liking. The answer was the Old London Road, which he constructed to divert the older road which came from Barnet. But he could not close it up completely—it was the King's highway and it remains so which is why the Verulam Golf Club was unable to close the footpath right of way across the golf course, from Longmire Road to the junction with Cottonmill Lane. The other footpaths which crossed it at right angles could be and were closed.

Perhaps some day it may form part of a pleasant river walk, to be added to the amenities of this part of the district. The Old London Road came into the town via Sopwell Lane, still picturesque with a fifteenth century house on the corner of Holywell Hill, once a public house (the Crown and Anchor), and now an antique shop. There is also an ancient inn called the Goat, which has been restored and turned into a useful centre for local society meetings, and another which specialises in folk music. It no longer has the large stables for which it was noted in the eighteenth century.

At the Old London Road end of Sopwell Lane, began one of the toll roads, with which the countryside was usefully dotted. The toll-house was opposite the junction with Sopwell Lane and the toll road ended at a toll-house at the junction of the two London Roads—where today Alma Road runs towards the north and the railway station. From this point runs the modern London Road—the St Albans portion of Telford's great achievement, the Holyhead Road. What's in a name? Certainly the blunt name, the A6, does not carry the romantic associations of 'The Holyhead Road', with its thoughts of Ireland, Wales and Gretna Green.

This last London Road was laid down at the turn of the 18-19th century. It cut through a high rise at the entrance to the town, and some houses were built above the new roadway, on the bank. Some on the south side were back to back, with the upper rooms of one house joined to the lower room of that on the street behind. Nearer the centre were some pleasant Regency houses with pretty iron verandahs. Most of these have now been demolished, but one remains, quite close to the Peahen, a Regency oasis in a desert of ordinary shops. The junction with Holywell Hill was cut between the Peahen and the Cross Keys, destroying the Cross Keys and both inn-yards. The name was transferred to the public house which, much reduced, took its place.

The next spoke of the 'road' wheel is to the north. This is Saxon in origin, and in Norman times was the eastern part of the mediaeval market. The western part is the modern Market Place with passages between there and Chequer Street marking the spaces between the stalls. These have gradually turned into lock-up shops and then the shopping streets we see today. This was completed by the late 14th century, and St Peter's Street boasted some houses by that time. There were some early side roads from St Peter's Street. Victoria Street started as Shropshire Lane, by which name it was known at the time of the Wars of the Roses; Catherine Street was earlier, dating almost certainly to the eleventh century, for St Catherine was the favourite saint of Abbot Geoffrey de Gorham, and there appears to be no other period of special interest in that lady.

The other side road from St Peter's Street was Cock Lane, now known as Hatfield Road. It is named after the ancient Cock Inn, at the south corner, when Hatfield Road was not much more than a cart track.

Until about the middle of the nineteenth century, Luton Lane, as Harpenden Road was called, went over Bernards Heath, from the lane now known as Waverley Road. It passed between the clay-pits which dotted the Heath and some brickmakers' cottages. These were 'restored' some years ago to become a charming house, no longer on the road. The old road is still here as a pathway joining the present main road at the traffic lights and crossing over to the prehistoric earthwork, Devil's Dyke on the other side of the crossroads.

ABOVE: The Clock Tower, 1787, and BELOW: with Semaphore, 1812.

LEFT: How the semaphore worked.

BELOW: High Street and Market Place 1812, and
RIGHT: in mid 19th century.

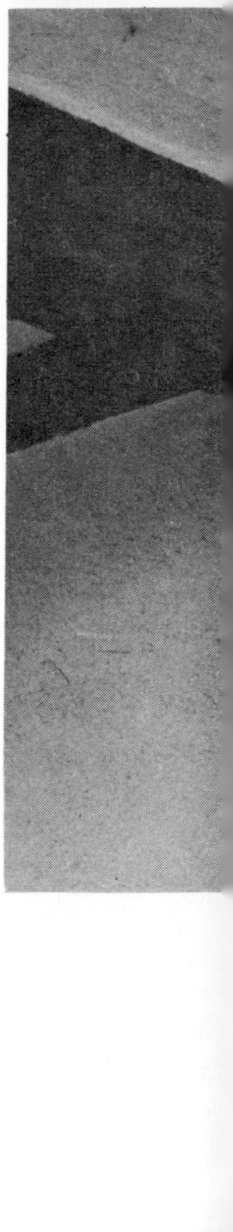

LEFT: High Street and Market Place today.

ABOVE: French Row and Christopher Inn, and BELOW: Bracket in Gateway, Christopher Inn.

RIGHT: Fleur de Lys Inn, and BELOW: Fleur de Lys Yard, 14th to 19th centuries.

Fleur de Lys

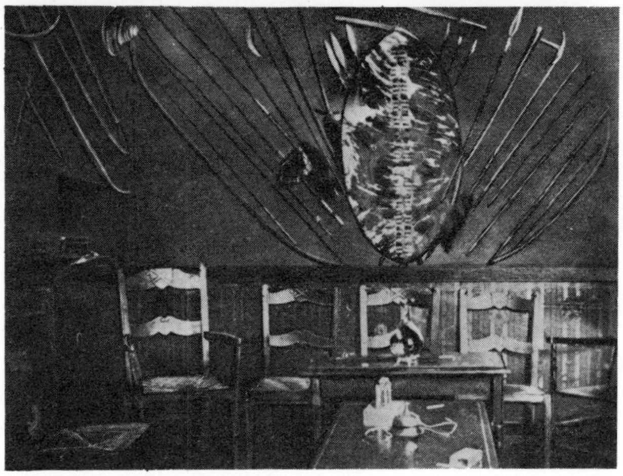

ABOVE: Oldest London Road, since Watling Street
(Marconi Instruments)

LEFT: Boot Inn.

RIGHT: Sovereign Way.

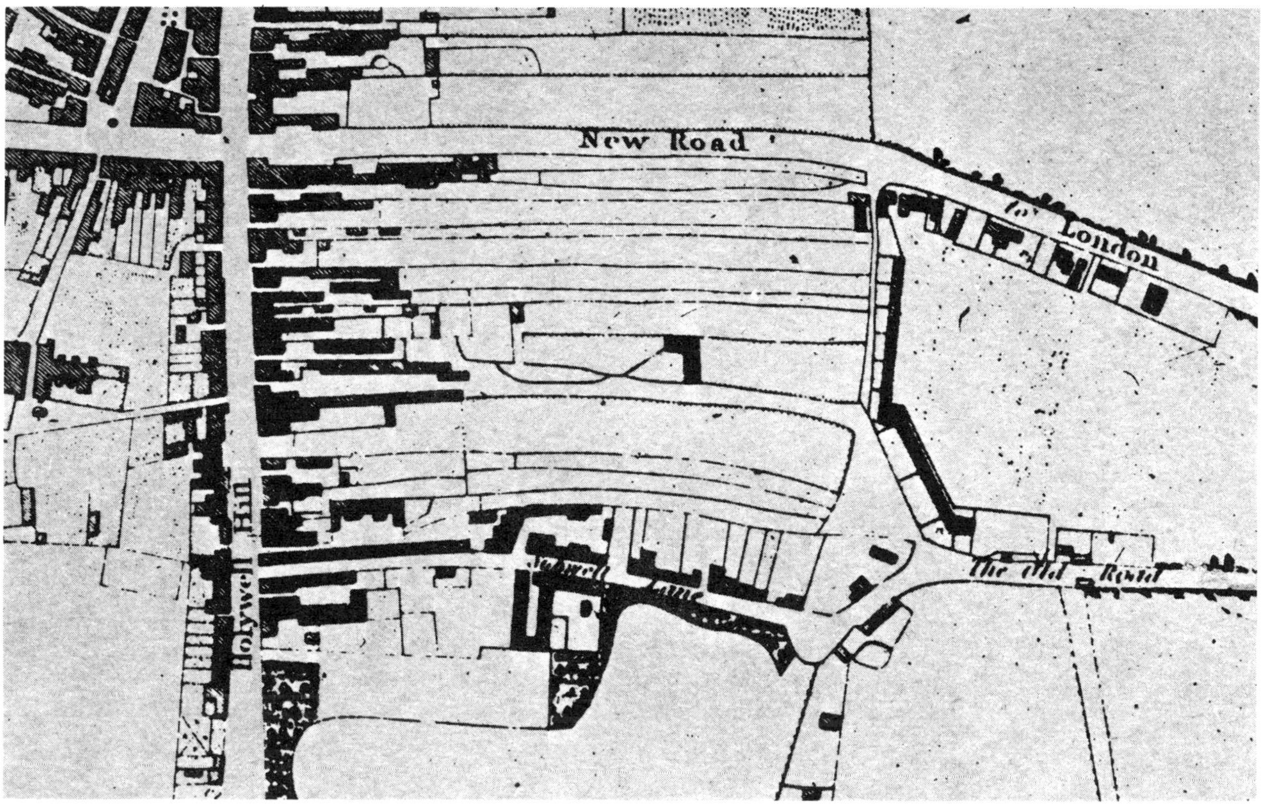

ABOVE: New London Road, late 18th cent.

BELOW: Fishpool Street (Marconi Instruments)

ABOVE: Lower end of Fishpool Street 1809, and BELOW: Fishpool Street, with the Little Red Lion. (Marconi Instruments)

ABOVE: Snowdrifts in London Road; the Liverpool Mail in trouble in 1812.

BELOW: Verulam Arms Inn, Verulam Road, *c* 1825, became a private house, then Bishop's Palace, finally Diocesan House.

ABOVE: A5 and A6 junction at Peahen crossroads in middle of St Albans; first pad-operated traffic lights in country.

BELOW: White Hart Hotel, mediaeval in origin.

ABOVE: Arrival of Simon, Lord Lovat at White Hart, on his way to London for trial and execution for treason, 1747.

LEFT: Sketch by Hogarth of Lord Lovat, at White Hart.
RIGHT: Fishpool Street. Gonnerston end.

ABOVE: The Market and St Peter's Street.

BELOW: Great Red Lion and 15th century Tudor Tavern.
(Marconi Instruments)

ABOVE LEFT: Angel Inn, now Manor Garden House, and RIGHT: Sign of the Angel, transferred to a bootshop in St Peter's Street.

BELOW LEFT: Fighting Cocks and RIGHT: George Inn.

ABOVE: New Turnpike Road, the improved road and St Albans about 1758.

CENTRE LEFT: Old tollgate in ruins, early 19th century, and RIGHT: the same viewpoint—20th cent. junction of old London Road and London Road. (Marconi Instruments)

BELOW: Sopwell Lane—Old London Road, superceded by New London Road, (A6). (Marconi Instruments)

In the Grand Manner

The most famous house in St Albans is Gorhambury. Its history goes back to the twelfth century, when Geoffrey de Gorham, a well-known Norman scholar, was appointed Abbot. He had come over to England to apply for the headship of the already well-known school, but had entered the Abbey a few years later. He was accompanied or followed by some kinsmen, to one of whom he had alienated the manor of Westwick, where on the ruins of a Roman Villa he constructed the first Gorhambury. This house was enlarged in the mediaeval period, and after the Dissolution, was acquired by a Merchant of the Staple, called Ralph Rowlatt, or Rowlett. The descendants of his daughters married into local families, one of which was that of John Jennings of Sandridge, whose son inherited some of the family property in St Albans. The Gorhambury building was sold to Sir Nicholas Bacon, Lord Keeper of the Great Seal. The house was old and inconvenient and Bacon rebuilt it on a slightly different site. There he entertained Queen Elizabeth, who was somewhat scornful of the size of the new building, saying, 'My Lord what a little house you have gotten,' to which he retorted, 'Madam my house is well, but you have made me too big for my house.' When she came again (she visited him at least four times), he had built a new wing with a long gallery of some 120 feet long and 18 feet wide. Her next visit was carefully costed at £577 6 7¼ for four days' entertainment.

Sir Nicholas's elder son, by his second marriage with Anne Cooke was Anthony, a delicate boy who never married, so the property passed to the younger son, Francis. He followed his father into the Law, becoming a Bencher of Gray's Inn, a Member of Parliament, and like his father, Keeper of the Great Seal (today's Lord Chancellor). He was one of the most brilliant men of a brilliant age, and it was said of him that when he was at Gorhambury, it was as if the Court had been there. In fact he was hopelessly extravagant, and despite marriage to a wealthy heiress, he died deeply in debt. He fell into disgrace, accused of taking bribes, and was impeached, the penalties being not to enter Parliament again, to be imprisoned—he served only a matter of days—and to pay a heavy fine. This he never settled, for he owed money to the King, which he never paid, and as the King was a prior creditor, other creditors were never paid either. He had retired to Gorhambury which he deeply loved and devoted himself among other hobbies, to gardening. He considered thirty acres the ideal plot. As the slope of the land prevented him from successfully moving water to fill a lake, he built a new house near Gorhambury. This proved so ruinously expensive to maintain that soon after his death it was demolished. He devoted his talents to writing, history, science and the famous Essays. His scientific theories, ahead of his time, were one of the influences which lay behind the foundation years later of the Royal Society for the Advancement of Science. His marriage was unhappy, and though his Will asked for him to be buried in St Michael's Church, there is no information as to where he came to rest. His kinsman and heir, Sir Thomas Meautys, was responsible for the fine memorial in the church, showing him resting in a chair. He left no children. A daughter of the Suffolk Bacons had married Meautys, and they became the owners. In 1652, Sir Harbottle Grimston, Master of the Rolls and a member of Parliament, bought Gorhambury from the executor of Meautys and married his widow, forging a link with the Bacon family. He brought his own collection of pictures which, with that of the Bacon family, made the combined collection outstanding. It includes four pictures of Sir Nathaniel Bacon, early examples of British portraiture. Included in the collection, but lent to the National Collection is the portrait of Edward Grimston, painted by Petrus Christus in 1446. It is the only fifteenth century English portrait having the date, the name of the painter, and the person represented equally well defined. There is also the oldest known English pile carpet, two windows of English painted glass from Tudor Gorhambury, and three contemporary painted terracotta busts of Sir Nicholas and Lady Anne Bacon with their son, Francis as a boy.

Gorhambury was rebuilt in 1777, when Sir Robert Taylor designed the present structure on a site some distance from the Tudor building, which was left to decay. The new Gorhambury was designed with a view to the better housing of the picture collections.

The other main great house is no longer in existence, but only disappeared in 1836, in order to widen and straighten Holywell Hill. A daughter of the Jennings family, a descendant of Ralph Rowlett, was born probably at Water End House near Sandridge, christened in the Abbey, and becoming a favourite of Princess Anne, married John Churchill, later Duke of Marlborough. Her name was Sarah Jennings, and she seems to have received Holywell House as part of her dowry. She and Marlborough made the house their home for many years, and in the fullness of time, she died there. The house was built by her ancestor, as a town house to add to his country house of Gorhambury but the property never returned to the Rowlatts, and the Earl Spencer, descendant of Sarah, owns property in St Albans today, notably the site of the City Museum. Holywell House was a pleasant enough Tudor building, but the north front, where the main entrance was altered and brought up to date at the time of Sarah's marriage, was plain early eighteenth century. The west front was parallel to Holywell Hill, and encroached on the roadway, forcing the road to make a bow to the west, now represented by Grove Road. When the main road was straightened, in 1835, the line of the road ran right through the west part of the building, which was demolished, and a new road and bridge were built. Sarah had always taken a great interest in the internal affairs of the town, as did her daughters, and daughters-in-law. One of these, Lady Spencer planted the cedar tree in the Sumpter Yard, and also the walk along the river way at the foot of the Abbey Orchard, known as Lady Spencer Grove. She also ran a charity school for girls, the Greencoat School, situated in Thorpe Road, adjoining the Entrance Gate of Holywell House. The school is no longer in existence, disappearing when Lady Spencer died. The great barn of Water End House, part of the premises of Brocket Hall, was taken down and re-erected on land behind St Peter's Street, and is a popular restaurant in the Civic Centre, run by one of the oldest families in the locality, the Thrales, whose pedigree can be traced to the fourteenth century.

Salisbury Hall, at London Colney, on the outskirts of St Albans, is a house whose history goes back to the ninth century. There are traces of the 15th century house built by the Earl of Salisbury, brother of Warwick the Kingmaker, who was probably staying in the house at the time of the First Battle of St Albans, 1455. Since that time many famous people have lived there. At one time the owner was Sir Jeremy Snow, friend of Charles II, who let the cottage adjoining to Nell Gwyn, to whom a son was born there, later created Duke of St Albans by his father, when he was fourteen. From 1905-1910 Lady Randolph Churchill lived in the house when her son, Winston was a boy, and later the house and property were used by De Havilland's aircraft firm who developed the famous Mosquito aeroplane. The prototype is preserved in a special hangar.

Mackerye End is a charming Tudor house near Harpenden, and Charles Lamb was related to the resident family and frequently visited. Tyttenhanger Park originated as a manor of St Albans Abbey, on which abbots built a private residence as a retreat from Abbey routine. At the Dissolution the property came into the possession of Sir Thomas Pope, founder of Trinity College, Oxford. His family retained possession until recently. The house was pulled down and rebuilt in the mid-sixteenth century. As time went on, it fell into disrepair, and was abandoned, but has now been bought and restored by a firm of famous architects for their own use. A great house now only known by its ruins is Sopwell Priory. At the Dissolution it came into possession of Sir Richard Lee, friend of Henry VIII, from whom he acquired all the domestic buildings of the monastery except the Abbey Church. Lee built the Mansion in St Peter's Street, which still stands, though with shops built into the ground floor and with the offices of a solicitor on the first floor. This was Lee's town house, but he decided to rebuild a good deal of Sopwell Priory as his country home. The ruins of today are part Priory and part Lee's Sopwell House.

St Michael's Manor was built by John Gape, an official of the Monastery before the Dissolution, who obtained the site and the Lordship of the manor. There he built himself a house, of which little more than one room remains, bearing an early Elizabethan date. The rest of the house was rebuilt in the 17th century. It became an hotel after the Second World War, and some alterations were made. When the site was threatened with development, which would have cut the Saxon monks' fishpond in several pieces, the City Council opposed the scheme and won the day.

There are a number of pleasant smaller historic houses in the borough. Kingsbury Manor is a late eighteenth century or Regency farmhouse. Darrowfield in St Michael's Street is an eighteenth century Dower House of Gorhambury. Bleak House (properly The Daltons) is Queen Anne, and houses the Social Services Department of the County Council. It has no connection with Charles Dickens. The Grange, from the late 18th century, is the Office of the chief officers of the City and District Council.

LEFT: Gorhambury: Edward Grimston, by Petrus Christie, 1446. Earliest known fully documented portrait of an Englishman. (From the Gorhambury Collection, by permission of the Earl of Verulam)

BELOW: Ruins of Nicholas Bacon's House, Gorhambury.

RIGHT AND OPPOSITE ABOVE: Terracotta Busts of Sir Nicholas, Lady Anne, and Francis Bacon as a boy. (From the Gorhambury Collection, by permission of the Earl of Verulam)

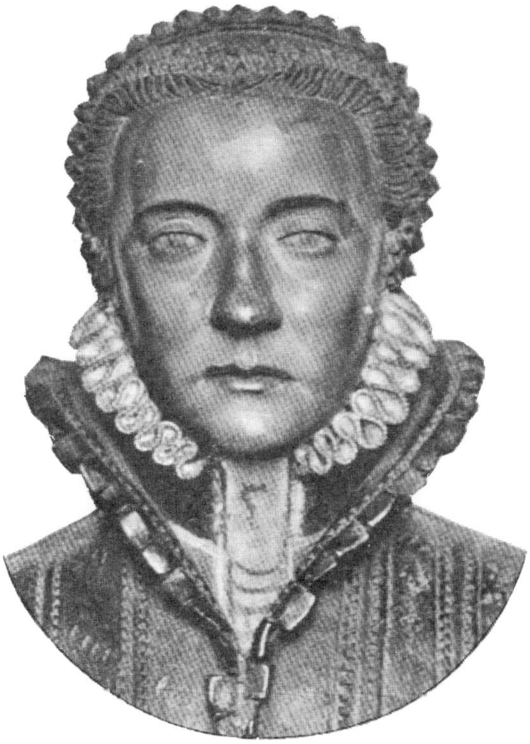 

LEFT: Francis Bacon as a man.

RIGHT: James Bucknell, 3rd Viscount Grimston, builder of present house.

ABOVE LEFT: Tudor Gor
today. (Both by pern

CENTRE: Hous

BELOW LEFT: Sir Thomas N
Lord Chancellor. (From (
of the

and RIGHT: Gorhambury
he Earl of Verulam)

Francis Bacon.

d RIGHT: Francis Bacon as
y collection by permission
rulam)

LEFT: Sarah, Duchess of Marlborough.

RIGHT: John Churchill, Duke of Marlborough.

BELOW: Waterend House, reputedly Sarah's birthplace.

ABOVE: Holywell House, St Albans; home of the Marlboroughs—demolished 1836.

LEFT: Holywell House, North Front.

RIGHT: St Michael's Manor, home of the Gape family, now an hotel.

ABOVE: Salisbury Hall dates back to the brother of Warwick the Kingmaker, and BELOW: Home of the Mosquito aeroplane.

ABOVE: Tyttenhanger Hall.

LEFT: Sopwell priory, granted to Sir Richard Lee at Dissolution.

RIGHT: The Mansion, Sir Richard Lee's town house.

LEFT: Mackerye End, connected with Charles Lamb.

RIGHT: House of Sir William Domville, whilom Lord Mayor of London.

BELOW: The Grange, about 1780, now offices of City and District Corporation.

ABOVE: Dr Cotton's College for the Insane.

LEFT: Bleak House (properly The Daltons), offices of the Social Services.

RIGHT: Shaw's Corner, Ayot St. Lawrence, home of George Bernard Shaw.

ERRATA

p.93. For LEFT read CENTRE; for RIGHT read BELOW

Printing: title page of Chronicle of St Albans,
printed by Wynkyn de Worde, 1528.

Craft and Commerce

From early times, industry of one sort or another was carried on in the district. The inhabitants of Verulamium dressed skins, and made cloth, which they sold to the Continent, and imported wines and fine pottery in return. Roman Verulam was a busy town with shops and businesses, provisions being brought in and sold in the market, just as today. Even Saxon St Albans was not a simple agricultural settlement; the monks brought civilisation and trade to the town. An inevitable early industry was transport. The Abbey forced the population into a certain sophistication and fostered education, which must have marked them off from the simple peasants of the neighbourhood. Specific industries flourished. The Abbey set the precedents, with the rise of a mediaeval equivalent to a publishing house, specialising in works of history, and the addition of a School of Art. St Albans installed the third printing machine in the country. The print shop was founded by John Insomuch, the Master of a School. His name is lost, and we know him by the nickname taken from the opening word of some of the books he printed. Although later on, his press closed down, it continued elsewhere, and the trade prospered again after the Reformation, from that time remaining a major industry here. One St Albans printer is responsible for producing many official Government documents, and the Salvation Army 'War Cry' also comes from a local press. The local Herts Advertiser has been issued since the eighteen-fifties, with an unrivalled collection of photographs. An early office was housed in a disused Nonconformist chapel but its present home is a modern one. The connected trade of bookbinding is also a local craft. The Bibles carried by the present Queen and her sister at the coronation of their father, King George VI were bound in St Albans.

One of the chief industries until the First World War was the manufacture of mens' straw 'boaters'. Straw plaiting was a local cottage industry in the sixteenth century, and little girls were taught the various plaits in 'plait schools', of which there were many in the town. One was in Waxhouse Lane and another in a cottage on the bank leading to the Abbey; only the step leading to the door remains. When the children could plait, they practised their craft alongside their mothers.

Machinery brought specialisation, and a common sight was that of women carrying large white bags, filled with bundles of straw-plait, which they took home to stitch on special sewing machines, returning the result to the factories. There the limp hat-shapes were dipped in glue, and put in presses, to be soaked with hot steam, and hung out in rows to dry and set, after which the women finishers took them over to sew in the linings, and add ribbon bands and bows. There were more than a dozen factories here, several of them quite large, and some in cottages. St Albans was said to make mens' boaters for the world, but then imported light straw from Japan ruined the trade, and finally the War killed the fashion for such hats. The trade in women's hats, never important to St Albans, continued in Luton, but declined when fashion changed and women took to going bareheaded too. Manufacturers went bankrupt, their factories closed down.

Another long established local industry was brewing. In the eighteenth century there were several breweries in the town. Searankes had breweries both in Hatfield and St Albans, and brewing flourished in the sixteenth century. In the nineteenth century there was Adey and White's brewery, where the Checquers car-park was later established. Until fire-engines were powered, it was always the great shirehorses of the brewery that were called out to draw the fire-apparatus. Another brewery was Kent's, behind Holywell Hill. These were the last to survive, while Kentish's had already disappeared. A Kentish was Mayor in the sixteenth century.

There were various mills from early times, three listed in Domesday Book. These belonged to the Abbey. The tenants of the Abbey were all required to grind their corn at the Abbey Mills, and when tenants wove their own cloth in their cottages, the cloth had to be treated at the Abbot's fulling-mill, a demand which frequently led to trouble between Abbot and town. After the Reformation the mills changed owners, and new ones emerged; run on water-power from the River Ver. One such was Kingsbury Mill, a corn-mill, which in recent years has become a museum. The Silk Mills, started in 1818 after many years of weaving silk cloth, turned to silk-reeling, later reeling artificial silk thread. The Sopwell Mill is now offices, and another mill is a private house, though during a severe storm a few years ago, the wheel woke up to try to do its own work, and nearly brought down the old casing as it nobly strove to turn once more.

Another industry which has disappeared is boot and shoe making. There were several boot makers with factories and several firms handled bespoke trade.

The most prominent trades today employ the makers of motor-cars, but their workpeople go to Vauxhall's at Luton. Similarly many are employed at the Hawker-Siddeley aviation works at Hatfield. An unusual industry is that of chronometer-making, at Mercer's, where marine instruments and clocks have been made for over a century, for the shipping of the world.

New industries have taken the place of those which have died out. One interesting development is that St Albans exports macaroni and pasta to Italy. Musical instruments have been made here since the Salvation Army set up a factory to make instruments for their own bands. Having blown hard, the bandsmen can quench their thirst with Rose's soft drinks, manufactured a short distance away.

A mile or so away is Rothamsted, a world-famous agricultural research station, and within the District's boundary are the office and research laboratories of the London School of Hygiene and Tropical Medicine.

NEW COATS and DRESSES.

VALUE IN HANDKERCHIEFS.

GLOVES and FUR SETS

ALWAYS POPULAR GIFTS.

ALL THE LATEST SHAPES IN FUR SETS

STYLISH MILLINERY.

XMAS PARTY BLOUSES.

EVERYTHING for the CHILDREN.

EIDER DOWN QUILTS.

NOVELTIES IN FANCY LINENS, COSEYS, Etc.

APRONS FOR PRESENTS.

Real Witney Blankets

PRESENTS FOR OUR Soldiers & Sailors AT HOME OR ABROAD

NOVELTIES for PRESENTS IN ART NEEDLEWORK DEPARTMENT.

A Large Stock of WOOLS IN KHAKI AND OTHER COLOURS.

SMART SHOES.

BEDROOM SLIPPERS.

EMBROIDERED BEDSPREADS.

DORELLS, HIGH STREET and THE ABBEY CLOISTER, ST. ALBANS.

ABOVE: Herts Advertiser Printing works.

BELOW: Advertising, 1914.

Mills: LEFT: Old flour-mill, Kingsbury, now a museum; RIGHT: Cotton-mill, early 19th cent.; BELOW: Abbey Mill, silk mill, early 19th cent.

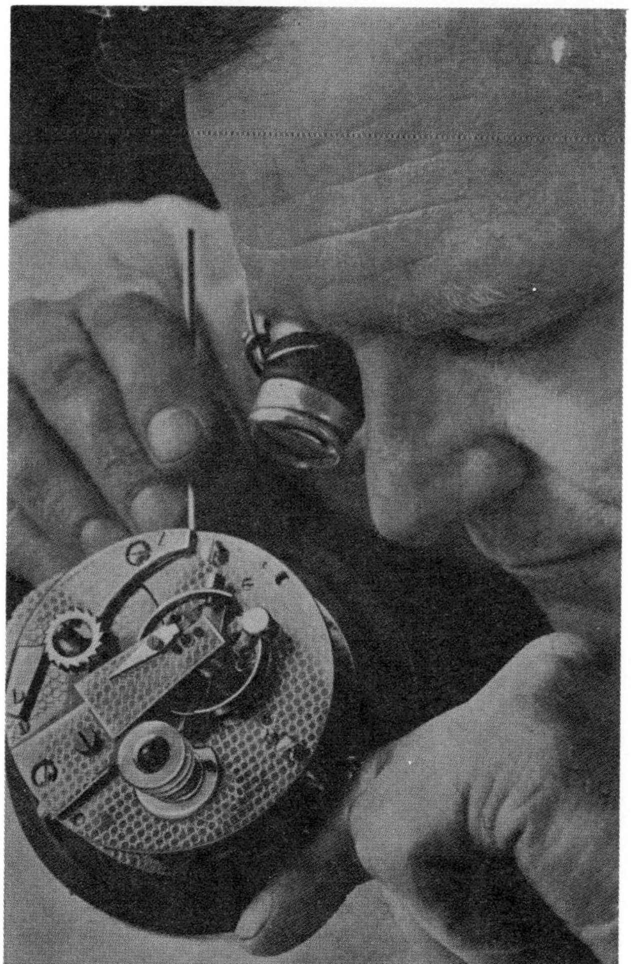

ABOVE: New Barnes mills, Sopwell.

LEFT: Marine Chronometer-making. (Mercer)

RIGHT: Telecommunication instruments. (Marconi)

LONDON AND NORTH WESTERN
RAILWAY.

OPENING
OF THE
ST. ALBANS BRANCH.

The Public are requested to take notice, that the St. Albans Branch Line, between

St. ALBANS and WATFORD,

Will be open for Passenger Traffic on

WEDNESDAY NEXT, MAY 5th.

LONDON TIME IS KEPT AT ALL THE STATIONS.

To Watford.

Distances from St. Albans	STATIONS.	WEEK DAYS.								
Miles	LEAVE	PAR A.M.	A.M.	NOON	P.M.	P.M.	P.M.			
...	ST. ALBANS	7.30	9. 5	12.55	3. 0	5.15	7.30		...	...
	ARRIVE AT									
1¾	PARK STREET	7.34		12.59	3. 4		7.34	...	...	..
3¼	BRICKETT WOOD	7.37	...	1. 2	3. 7	...	7.37	...	...	.
6¼	WATFORD	8.10	9.19	1.15	3.20	5.29	7.48	...	..	..
24¼	LONDON	9.15	10. 0	2. 0	4. 0	6.10	8.15	...	...	

From Watford.

STATIONS.	WEEK DAYS.								
LEAVE	PAR A.M.	A.M.	P.M.	P.M.	P.M.	P.M.			
LONDON	7.30	9.45	1. 0	3.30	5.15	8. 0	..		
WATFORD	8.20	10.20	1.40	4.10	5.45	8.35	...		
ARRIVE AT									
BRICKETT WOOD	8.27		1.47	4.17		8.42		..	...
PARK STREET	8.31	...	1.51	4.21	...	8.46	...	...	...
ST. ALBANS	8.40	10.35	2. 0	4.30	6. 0	8.55	...	...	...

PASSENGERS' FARES.

STATIONS	St. Albans					Park Street					Brickett Wood					Watford				
	1st Class	2nd Class	3rd Class	Return 1 Cl.	Return 2 Cl.	1st Class	2nd Class	3rd Class	Return 1 Cl.	Return 2 Cl.	1st Class	2nd Class	3rd Class	Return 1 Cl.	Return 2 Cl.	1st Class	2nd Class	3rd Class	Return 1 Cl.	Return 2 Cl.
	s. d.	s. d.	s. d.	s. d.	s. d.	s. d.	s. d.	s. d.	s. d.	s. d.	s. d.	s. d.	s. d.	s. d.	s. d.	s. d.	s. d.	s. d.	s. d.	s. d.
ST. ALBANS	...	...	...		..	0 6	0 4	0 ¼	0 9	0 6	0 6	0 4	0 3	0 9	0 6	1 0	0 8	0 4½	1 6	1 0
PARK STREET	0 6	0 4	0 1½	0 9	0 6			..			0 6	0 4	0 1½	0 9	0 6	0 6	0 4	0 4	0 9	0 8
BRICKETT WOOD	0 6	0 4	0 3	0 9	0 6	0 6	0 4	0 ¼	0 9	0 6	..	...	...	..	..	0 6	0 4	0 3	0 9	0 6
WATFORD	1 0	0 8	0 4½	1 6	1 0	0 6	0 4	0	0 9	0 6	0 6	0 4	0 3	0 9	0 6	.	..	.	.	.
LONDON	3 6	2 6	2 0	4 3	3 6	...		.	...	...	..	.			..	3 0	2 0	1 5½	4 0	2 4

Two Intermediate Stations, Brickett Wood and Park Street, will be opened. Persons wishing to proceed b[y] [th]e Trains must be on the Platform waiting for the Arrival of the Trains timed to Stop at these places. The Guard wi[ll] [is]sue the Tickets, and each Person is requested to have the exact amount of Fare ready.

[G]eneral Manager's Office,
Euston Station, May 1st, 1858.

By Order,

MARK HUISH

Railways.

Play the Game

The Abbey Theatre, built through the enthusiasm of the dedicated Company of Ten, started in a home-built theatre-club in the grounds of the never-to-be-forgotten Cyril Swinson, and now inhabits the first theatre built in St Albans since the fine open air theatre built by the Romans, not far away so many centuries before. The gap between was filled by travelling companies, performing in inn-yards, like the Queen's, and by the poor little County Theatre, on the site of today's Marks and Spencer's. Steeple-chasing began on Nomansland common, and was continued in Gorhambury Park for some years, fostered by a retired jockey, called Coleman, who was licensee of the Queen's Hotel which he re-named the Turf Hotel. We have, too, a legend that cricket began in Charles II's reign with the first (or more likely a very early) Cricket Club here. Some even go so far as to claim that the Merry Monarch himself wielded a strong swipe with the willow. Anyway, one can play most field games in Clarence Park, Verulamium Park, Batchwood golf course (which belongs to the corporation) and the Verulam Golf Club (which doesn't). Then one can swim at Westminster Lodge, and practise athletics. The City Football Team are appropriately known as the Saints.

The old sport of coaching flourished from the time it was a utilitarian means of transport, and we see its aquatic descendants on the lake at Verulamium in the form of model power-boat racing and model aeroplanes. For the music lovers, the City Hall fills a long-felt want, and a chance to hear great orchestras, and in the Abbey there is a magnificent organ.

When the city started to grow, there was a small public Library, to serve a population of 17,000. Then Andrew Carnegie gave us a new one, a pioneer in the practice of open access to the shelves. Since then we have built two branch libraries, and were among the first authorities to invest in a mobile library to take books to the readers.

Appropriately, the Architectural and Archaeological Society have flourished for some hundred years, watching over our treasures, and the newer Civic Society, founded in 1962, reinforces our care that the environment shall not be ruined as so many towns have found to their cost.

Celebrated ALES
HORSE.

ABOVE LEFT: Batchwood Hall, the Municipal Golf Course.

CENTRE: Cyril Swinson: inspired Company of Ten, wrote Scenarios of St Albans, 1948 and 1953.

BELOW: St Peter's Street, site of County Theatre behind ivy-clad building; gave way to Marks and Spencer, about 1960.

RIGHT: Coaching about 1870.

School in Lady Chapel (Drawing by F. G. Kitton)

A Degree of Learning

St Albans School is one of the oldest educational foundations in the country. It started in Saxon times. Early in the Norman period, it was well-known and well esteemed outside this country, so much so that when the headship was vacant, a distinguished Norman scholar made plans to apply for the vacancy. His name was Geoffrey de Gorham. Unfortunately his journey was held up for some time because of heavy weather in the Channel, and he found on arrival that the post had been filled. He had been attracted by the conditions of service. The school was not a monastery school; the Master was never a monk and was apparently independent of the Abbot; he could be a married man, and his pupils were the sons of local petty gentry, merchants and prosperous tradesmen, who as a rule paid fees. In the fourteenth century, the Abbot gave money to found scholarships for a certain number of able boys. Some lads came from other parts of the country as boarders, one from as far as Wales. The Master had the monopoly of education within the Liberty of the Abbey, and so high was the reputation of the School for learning that the Master apparently awarded a form of degree in the late thirteenth century, at the time when another University was essaying to set up, first in Stamford, and finally at Cambridge. Had it not been for the presence of the Abbey, St Albans might have been the new university, but another strong competitor to Oxford would not have suited in the immediate neighbourhood. De Gorham liked the set-up so much that he went on to Dunstable and started up a similar school in advance of the foundation of the Priory. Gorham was an original teacher and wrote a play based on the life of his favourite saint, St Catherine, for his boys to perform. This is said to be the first allusion to drama in England. To dress the performance he borrowed the valuable copes worn by the St Albans monks on ceremonial occasions. They were taken to his house for safety at night and an outbreak of fire destroyed them all, and de Gorham, devastated by the disaster entered the Abbey as a monk in expiation. In 1119 he was unanimously elected Abbot. One of his relations was the builder of the first Gorhambury.

The most famous Old Boy of the School came from an estate belonging to the Abbey at Abbot's Langley. His father became a monk after the death of his wife, and his uncle was also in the Abbey. As no other school was allowed, the boy, Nicholas Breakspear, must have been a scholar there, but when he, at a suitable age, applied to join his father and uncle, the Abbot examined him and failed him as not coming up to standard. He left the country and finished his education on the Continent, eventually becoming in 1154 the only Englishman to become Pope. He chose the name of Adrian IV, showing clearly his affection for his native home. The School must have been successful, for Lollards in the fourteenth century felt it to be worthwhile to flood the town with handbills advocating reforming opinions, which shows a gratifying sense of literacy among the ordinary folk. Wills, too, prove that many inhabitants possessed books before the advent of the Schoolmaster printer. The School was closed by the Royal Commissioners in 1539, but the ex-Abbot obtained Letters Patent, with permission to set up a Free School, with Master, Usher and Chaplain. It is not known what happened. When the first Charter was granted, the new owners of the Abbey Church took the sensible course of using the Lady Chapel for the School instead of demolishing it as redundant. A passage was constructed to close off the Lady Chapel, with openings at each end, and this remained until the boys transferred to the Great Gateway in 1871.

During the Tudor period, the School gradually built up to about a hundred boys. Sir Nicholas Bacon took great interest in its progress, and its struggling finances were helped by the rent of Licences to sell wine—the Wine Licences, of Elizabeth and James I, and the existing documents describe the financial and educational struggles. The roll diminished by 1740 to some forty pupils. The School belonged to the Corporation, which could not charge fees, and the Master was the incumbent of a parish church, taking local or boarding pupils in his house, and the few free pupils were neglected, and diminished to nothing.

After 1900, the numbers grew again, and in the second decade of the century, it was realised that new buildings had become necessary. Today there are in the region of 800 boys.

To take the place of the neglected Free School, during the nineteenth century, there was a Charity School, which gave some clothing as well as teaching, and whose finances came largely from an annual sermon preached in the Abbey, and the resulting collection and donations. At the same time, there was a charity school run by the Baptists in Dagnall Street. They also gave clothing as well as tuition. Early in the nineteenth century, the Abbey National School opened in Spicer Street, and some of the charity schools closed down. A Greencoat School for girls had been opened by Lady Spencer in Thorpe Road, and lasted until its patroness died; another similar Bluecoat school depended on the charity of Lady Verulam, which lasted rather longer than Lady Spencer's.

The several Board Schools which followed the education Act of 1870, became County Council Schools in 1902, but for some years there was no Grammar School for Girls; a Grammar School for boys supplemented the free places at the St Albans School. A third (mixed) Grammar School was named after Francis Bacon. After the Second World War, the St Albans senior schools 'went Comprehensive', apart from the St Albans School, and the Girls High School, which had started as a school of the Girls Public Day School Trust.

The St Albans School of Art in new premises, and the St Albans College of Further Education, with the Hertfordshire College of Building, are all flourishing.

ABOVE: College of Further Education.

CENTRE: The Grammar School Hall.

BELOW: One end of passage through Abbey.

LEFT: School and Gateway.

BELOW: Experimental Station, Rothamstead, 1847.

RIGHT: The Library—an early picture.

Charters of Liberty

Popular government in St Albans began, like everywhere else in the country, with Magna Carta in 1215. The original meeting of the Great Council, the first to which any representatives of the common members of the public were summoned, met in St Albans in 1213, and there the first draft of the Great Charter was drawn up and read to the assembly. The Abbey was the premier abbey in the country and the Charter became the authority to which writers on the constitution of this country appealed. There was, of course, no Town Charter until the Abbey was dissolved. The Abbey was from the first the owner and the ownership was established by gifts, legacies and purchases. Some of the gifts came from wealthy donors, some of them Royal, some from local people while some were from wealthy monks who gave them on joining the monastic community. Such a one was Robert, Earl of Northumberland, who gave the land on which was constructed the Priory of Tynemouth, a daughter-house of St Albans. Robert became a monk, one of the large number who built up the aristocratic tradition of the community at St Albans.

Many towns on Royal or lay lands acquired charters of liberty at the time of the Crusades. The necessity for cash was not great in the Middle Ages when most of the income of landowners was derived from dues in kind—so many eggs at Christmas and so on. But the necessity for hard cash which the foreign wars introduced changed the economic habits of nations and reacted on their political life. The merchant class were growing in wealth and became the source of funds to fit out armies. Landowners had to give some quid pro quo to the men with the money, so charters of liberty were demanded and sold. Many towns at that time became remarkably free, but there were no charters for monastic towns. As the Church never died, its lands were never sold to lay owners who might be more open-minded and readier to grant charters. So however wealthy and sophisticated the population of a monastic town might be, no chance for political advance existed, until the power of the religious houses was broken. So, in St Albans there was no town council until the Tudors. Then things moved rapidly, though the first charter did not come until the mid-century.

Henry VIII took the lands and other possessions of the monastery, giving or selling the property by degrees. Some of the landed property was still in the hands of the King in 1545, notably what came to be known as the Moot Hall in the Market Place, which was handed over in 1553 to the new corporation for a Town House or Town Hall. It was to serve this purpose for some three hundred years. A charter with leave to set up a corporation with a Mayor was granted by Edward VI.

Until this grant, it is uncertain who ruled the town after the disappearance of the Abbey Rule, but probably the most prominent citizens took upon themselves the administration of the borough. Some practice had been gained by a body who managed the Clock House or Clock Tower, which had never been a possession of the Abbey, but had probably been built by a mixture of public subscription and private generosity. It was run by a varying number of 'feoffees', in other words, a committee, which at one time numbered as many as nearly one hundred members. It would appear that the influential citizens, denied self-government by the autocratic Abbey, and anxious to have a modicum of power, had seized on the chance of ruling something outside the power of the Abbey, and having served an apprenticeship in this way, had slipped into the vacuum left by the dissolution of the monastery. They carried on until the Edward VI charter, fourteen years after the Abbots vanished. Whether there was any active participation by the Government in any of the affairs of the town before this charter is doubtful, but local government went on apparently without interference and was presumably carried on by ad hoc committees without legal authority but with the weight of general consent. The charter, when it came, was obviously operated by much the same personnel, and the hiatus seems to have been more theoretical than practical. In reality it gave legal basis for what was already in existence. In any case, St Albans had lost a great deal of its importance when the Abbey regime vanished, and in place of a despotic Abbot there remained a mere Rector, an employee of the new Council. St Albans seems to have slipped easily into the position of an unimportant market-town situated on an important and busy road.

The various charters established the pattern of local government in St Albans until the Municipal Reform Act in 1835, and then successive Acts extended the suffrage to all qualified citizens. Early polls were held in public, the polling booths being set up in the space in front of the Clock Tower and the poll declared from the hustings.

The first charter gave to the town a building which had belonged to the monastery and had apparently served as a court room. This was in future to be a Town House or Town Hall. It served this purpose for over two centuries. It stood in the Market Place, and the ground floor was the Compter prison and also housed the moveable stocks and pillory. Upstairs was a large all purpose room. It was big enough later on to entertain 200 guests at dinners, according to entries in Mayors' Accounts, of which some examples survive. The borough court was held there, but the County Justices usually sat in the large room over the Great Gateway.

By the charter of Edward VI, the town was made a free borough, ruled by a Mayor assisted by ten of the 'discreeter and better men' with a Steward, Chamberlain and two Sergeants-at-Arms. A Court was to be held every Wednesday and the Mayor and Steward were to sit as magistrates. This Bench, separate from the County Justices, remained until the latter half of the twentieth century when it was amalgamated with the County Bench. Two weekly markets and three annual fairs were granted. The Abbey Church, which had been bought from the King by the burgesses, became the Abbey Parish Church, with the advowson the property of the corporation, as it remained until the Municipal Reform Act of 1835, by which it became unlawful for a council to own a parish church. Queen Mary I confirmed this charter, though the original has vanished. Elizabeth I confirmed both charters in 1560. She also granted a Wine Charter in 1570 to help the finances of the School by letting two licenses for burgesses to sell wines, the money to go to the School. A second Wine Charter was granted by James I, which permitted three licences. A charter of Charles I elucidated the previous one and allowed the appointment of twenty-four Assistants to enlarge the council. A High Steward was to hold a life-office and a Recorder was to be appointed.

The next charter the borough received was of Charles II in 1664 with a fine portrait of the King looking far from 'merry'. The Common Council was to consist of twelve Principal Burgesses, henceforth to be known as Aldermen. When James II acceded to the throne, he altered the charters of many boroughs, including those of London and St Albans, in his effort to return the country to the Catholic faith. He realised that his policy would fail with the counties; the country gentlemen were too independent to be intimidated by the Court, but he was more successful with the borough members. In 1685 the Council Minutes record that by a new charter, the Council was increased by a number of new members who were not even inhabitants of the borough. Even the next Mayor came from Tring, as not enough eligible Tories could be found in St Albans, and the new Mayor had to appoint a deputy with full powers. This charter was declared void when William III and Mary ascended the throne, James II ran away, and the Charles II charter was restored.

The old Town Hall had become dilapidated and inconvenient. Both borough and Quarter Sessions wanted new premises, but they wanted different sites. The Justices wanted a site in Romeland, and asked for it every Quarter Sessions, and were refused as regularly. The Council could buy slum property in the north of the Market Place cheaply, and refused to spend unnecessary money. The argument went on for several years, but at last the present site was agreed, and then they argued about payment and ownership of the premises.Finally the finance needs were split as two-thirds from the Justices and one-third from the town. The strange result—that the town did not own its Town Hall, but paid rent for it—led to controversy in the mid-twentieth century, when the County to whom the Justices' rights had passed needed a newer, larger law-court and other County buildings, and proposed that they should use sites in the town's new Civic Centre to build a new police station, law-courts and other County buildings. They offered to sell the old town hall to the borough, at what seemed an outrageous price, take the George Smith listed building off the protected list and permit the building of a supermarket. Fortunately, outraged public opinion stopped this damage to environment and the visual amenities of St. Albans, and Counsel's opinion confirmed that the borough had inalienable rights in a large portion of the building, and a deal was struck. The city bought out the County and in return the County acquired land which was freehold property of the city. Once more peace reigned.

Until 1870, bribery was a regular feature of elections and was generally accepted, but the corruption which characterised elections in St Albans was exceptional and shocked even the morals of the eighteenth century. By the middle of the nineteenth, Parliament took note of it, and the borough was forced to face a Commission of Enquiry in 1852, the result of which was that St Albans lost its individual Member of Parliament, and had to share a member with one of the County constituencies. As the electorate increased, successive re-distribution of seats altered the location of members, and the position of the city altered with them, until now the city is almost back to its pre-1852 position, with an individual Member of Parliament.

The last charter of the old borough was that of Victoria in 1877. The Abbey had become a Cathedral, and consequently the borough became a City. Under that Charter St Albans was organised until the great shake-up in 1974 of Local Government, whereby the old boundaries were revised and some parts of the country found themselves with strange bedfellows. The City of St Albans joined with the St Albans Rural District, and the Urban District of Harpenden, and after some discussion the name of the new set-up was agreed as 'The City and District of St Albans'. The last election of the City Council was held in May 1973, and James Greening became the last Mayor of the City. So ended a line of Mayors, some good, some not so good. In 1974 a new Council was elected, considerably larger than its predecessors—54 members instead of 28, no Aldermen, and at first a Chairman instead of a Mayor. Very soon, however, authority was given for it to be entitled a City and to have a Mayor, who took on the trappings of the Mayoralty—red fur-trimmed robe, gold chain and badge and all, with silver-gilt mace of Charles II's date carried on the shoulder of the Mace-bearer and placed in front of the Mayor in solemn ceremony when the Council is in session. Those of us who cared deeply for the ancient City were glad to see that some of the connection with the past and a little of its colour and tradition had been kept to remind the citizens that all has not been thrown into the dustbin, and that something is still left of a past which has had its great moments. We are still in St Albans. Floreat Civis Albani.

ABOVE: The Town Hall.

BELOW: Early 19th cent. election.

The Charters: Edward VI, 1553; Elizabeth I, Wine Charters (p.116); Charles I (p.117); Victoria (p.119).

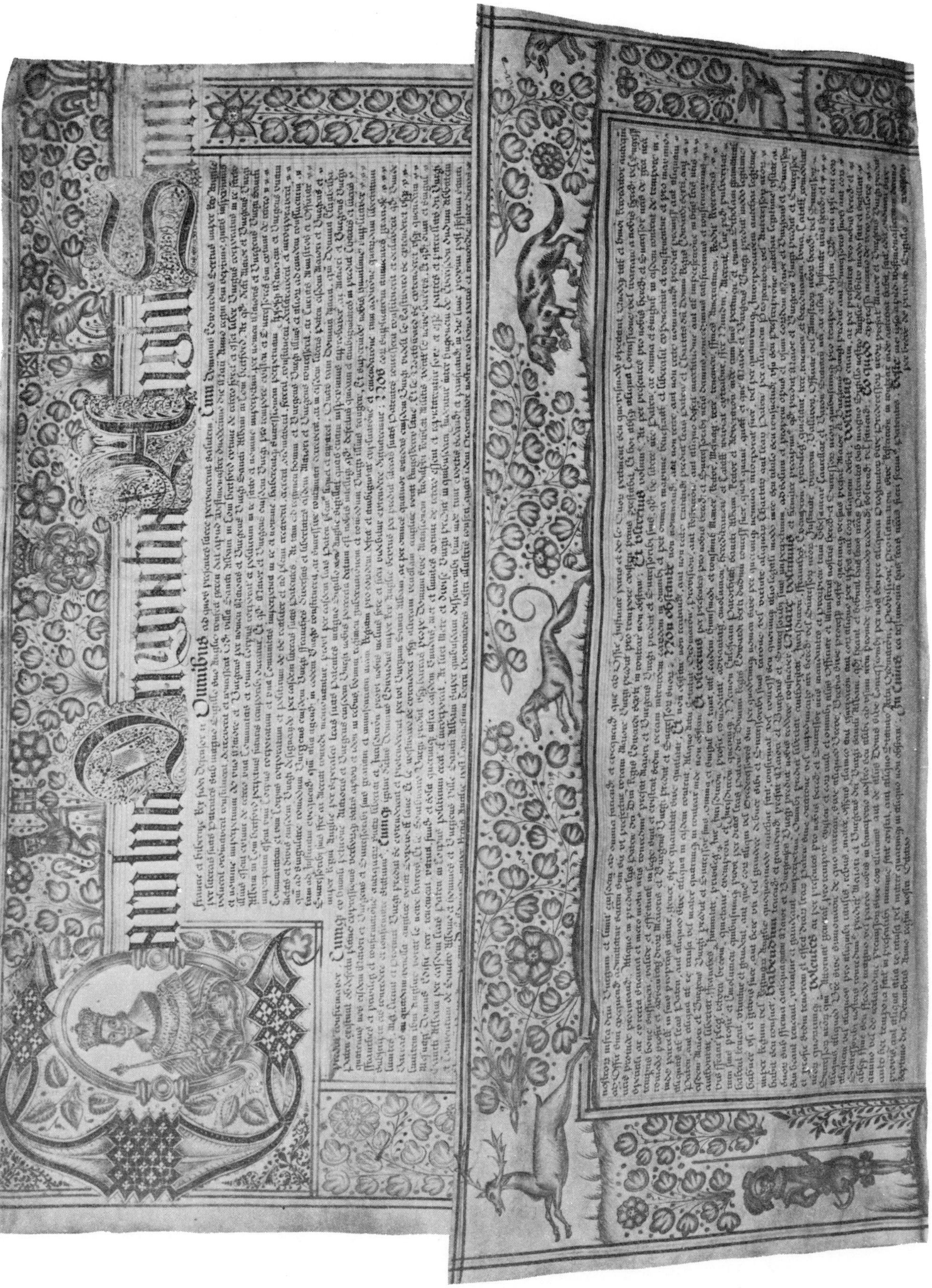

Charles II's Portrait from the 1664 Charter.

Victoria by the Grace of God

of the United Kingdom of Great Britain and Ireland Queen Defender of the Faith To all to whom these Presents shall come Greeting Whereas the Mayor Aldermen and Burgesses of the Borough of Saint Albans in Our County of Hertford have by their Petition under their Common Seal bearing date the twentieth day of June now last past humbly represented unto Us that by an Act of Parliament passed in the thirty eighth and thirty ninth years of Our Reign entituled "An Act to amend the Acts relating to the Ecclesiastical Commissioners and to enable them to carry into effect a certain proposal for the re-arrangement of the Dioceses of London Winchester and Rochester and the creation of a new Bishopric of Saint Albans" and thereon the fourth day of June one thousand eight hundred and seventy seven in accordance with the Letters Patent granted by Us the Lord Bishop of Saint Albans was duly invested and enthroned at Saint Albans the said Mayor Aldermen and Burgesses of the Borough of Saint Albans humbly prayed that We would be pleased to grant Letters Patent to constitute the aforesaid Borough of Saint Albans a City which We are minded to do Now therefore Know Ye that We of Our especial grace and favour and mere motion by these Our Royal Charter Will ordain constitute declare and appoint that Our said Borough of Saint Albans shall henceforth for the future and for ever hereafter be a City and shall be called and styled "The City of Saint Albans in the County of Hertford" instead of the Borough of Saint Albans and it shall have all and such liberties privileges and immunities as are incident to a City And We further declare and direct that the said Mayor Aldermen and Burgesses of Our said Borough of Saint Albans shall henceforth and by virtue of this Our Royal Charter be one Body Politic and Corporate by the name and style of "The Mayor Aldermen and Citizens of the City of Saint Albans" with all such and the same powers and privileges as they have hitherto had as the Mayor Aldermen and Burgesses of the Borough of Saint Albans and as if they had been incorporated by the name of the Mayor Aldermen and Citizens of the City of Saint Albans instead of the Mayor Aldermen and Burgesses of the Borough of Saint Albans In witness whereof We have caused these Our Letters to be made Patent Witness Ourself at Our Palace at Westminster the twenty eighth day of August in the fortyfirst year of Our Reign.

By Her Majesty's Command

Cardew

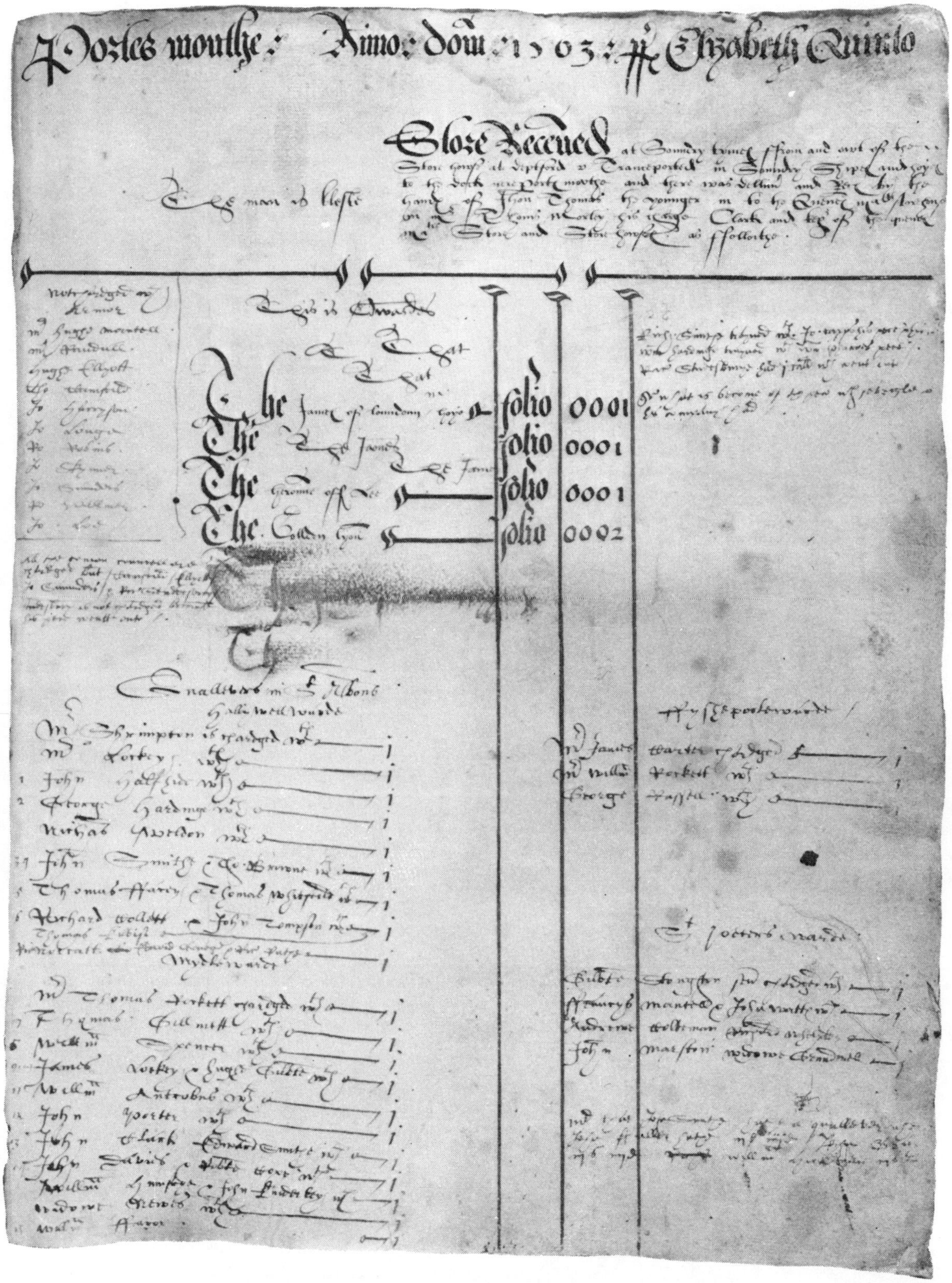

First entry in Corporation Minutes, 1563.

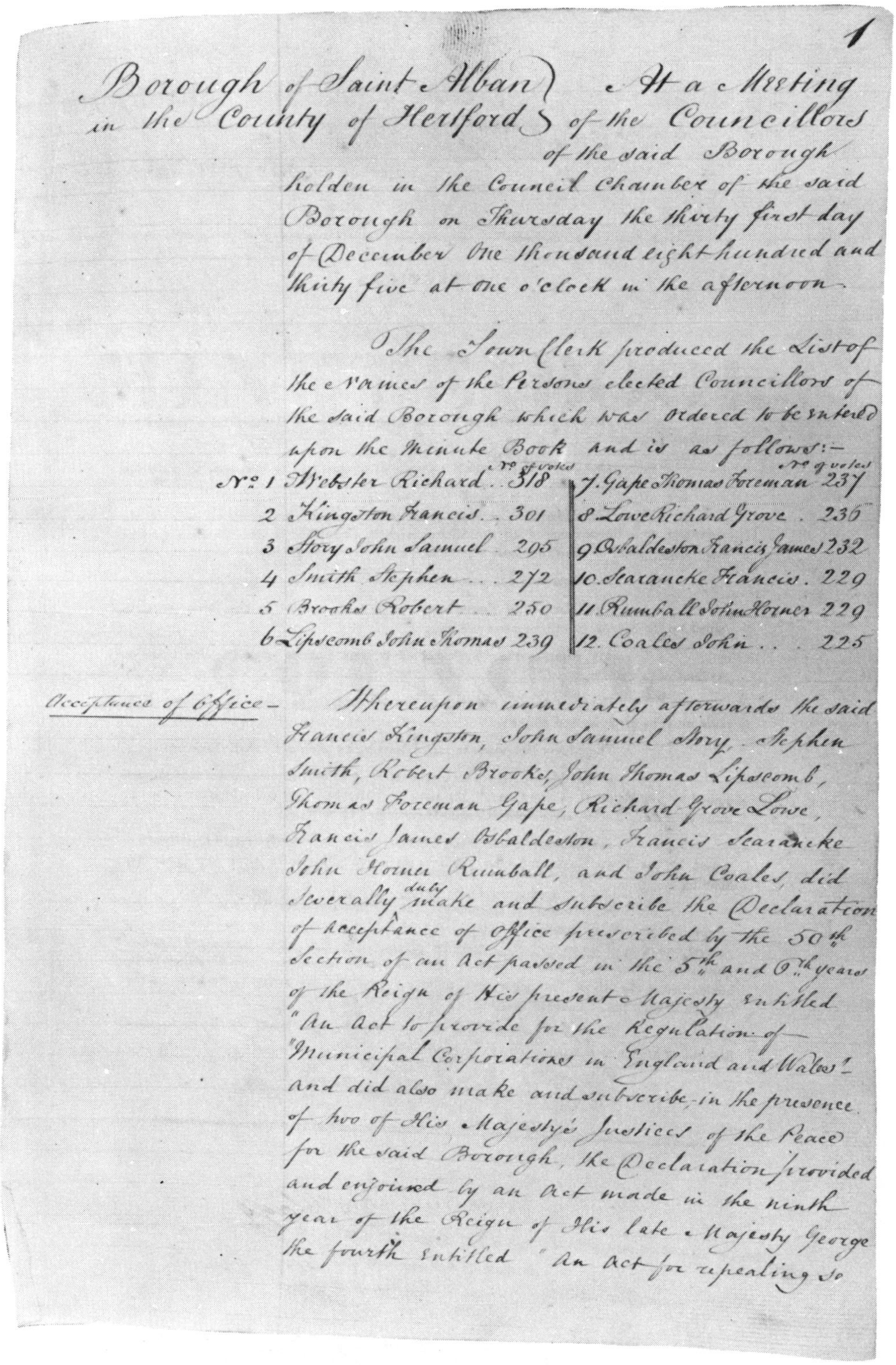

1

Borough of Saint Alban in the County of Hertford } At a Meeting of the Councillors of the said Borough holden in the Council Chamber of the said Borough on Thursday the thirty first day of December One thousand eight hundred and thirty five at one o'clock in the afternoon

The Town Clerk produced the List of the Names of the Persons elected Councillors of the said Borough which was ordered to be entered upon the Minute Book and is as follows:—

		No. of votes		No. of votes
No. 1	Webster Richard	318	7. Gape Thomas Foreman	237
2	Kingston Francis	301	8. Lowe Richard Grove	236
3	Story John Samuel	295	9. Osbaldeston Francis James	232
4	Smith Stephen	272	10. Searancke Francis	229
5	Brookes Robert	250	11. Rumball John Horner	229
6	Lipscomb John Thomas	239	12. Coales John	225

Acceptance of Office — Whereupon immediately afterwards the said Francis Kingston, John Samuel Story, Stephen Smith, Robert Brookes, John Thomas Lipscomb, Thomas Foreman Gape, Richard Grove Lowe, Francis James Osbaldeston, Francis Searancke John Horner Rumball, and John Coales, did severally duly make and subscribe the Declaration of Acceptance of Office prescribed by the 50th Section of an Act passed in the 5th and 6th years of the Reign of His present Majesty entitled "An Act to provide for the Regulation of "Municipal Corporations in England and Wales". and did also make and subscribe, in the presence of two of His Majesty's Justices of the Peace for the said Borough, the Declaration provided and enjoined by an Act made in the ninth year of the Reign of His late Majesty George the fourth entitled "An Act for repealing so

Start of first of Minutes 1835, after Municipal Reform Act.
(Charters & Minutes—Verulamium Museum)

Magna Carta Celebration: ABOVE LEFT: Guard of Honour; and BELOW: Master Of Rolls; ABOVE RIGHT: Magna Carta in the Abbey; and CENTRE: The Procession returns to City Hall.

BELOW RIGHT: Civic leaders at Dagnall Street Church.

ABOVE: Mayoral procession, 19th cent.

BELOW: A Royal occasion. The Queen-Mother receives the Freedom of St Albans, April 1961.

ABOVE: Chief Officers of City and District: Seated L to R: John Jeffrey, District Secretary; Betty Entwistle; John McKenna, Chief Technical Officer; Leslie Lowe, Chief Public Health Officer; Standing L to R: John Snowden, Chief Housing Officer; Ken Fletcher, Chief Planning Officer; Robert Pringle, Chief Recreation Officer; Clifford James, Treasurer.

LEFT: The City Mace and Seal.

RIGHT: City Gaol; black flag showing to indicate an execution, 1899.

Corporation Plate: The Robotham Cup 1603-4;
The Standing Dish 1604-5; The Grace Cup 1608-9.

Bibliography

Hertfordshire

Chauncy, *Sir* H. The Historical antiquities of Hertfordshire. 1700.

Clutterbuck, R. The History and antiquities of the County of Hertford. 3 vols. 1815-1827.

Cussans, J. E. History of Hertfordshire. 3 vols. 1870-1881.

Domesday Book. Text and translation edited by John Morris. 1976.

Hertfordshire Countryside Illustrated Magazine. 1946 to date.

Johnson, W. B. Industrial archaeology of Hertfordshire. 1970.

Pevsner, N. The Buildings of England: Hertfordshire. 1953.

Royal Commission on Historical Monuments (England). An Inventory of the historical monuments in Hertfordshire. 1910.

Salmon, N. The History of Hertfordshire. 1728.

Urwick, W. Non-conformity in Herts. 1884.

Victoria County History: Hertfordshire. 4 vols. 1902-1974.

Wray, M. *and others*. Location of industry in Hertfordshire: planning and industry in the post-war period. 1974.

St Albans

Ashdown, C. H. The Battles and battlefields of St Albans. 1455-1461. n.d.

Ashdown, C. H. St Albans historical and picturesque. 1893.

Association for Planning and Regional Reconstruction. A Social and economic survey of St Albans City. 1946.

The Boke of St Albans 1486. Facsimile ed. 1901.

Frere, S. Verulamium excavations. Vol. 1. 1972.

Gibbs, A. E. The Corporation records of St Albans. 1890.

Great Britain: Department of the Environment. List of buildings of special architectural and historic interest. City of St Albans, Hertfordshire. 1971.

Mason, F. B. Gibbs' illustrated handbook to St Albans.

Page, W. St Albans. 1920.

St Albans and Hertfordshire Architectural and Archaeological Society. Transactions. 1884-1914. 1924-1938. 1953 to date.

St Albans Civic Society. The River Ver at St Albans. 1968.

Shaw, S. G. *publisher*. History of Verulam and St Albans. 1815.

Swift, C. R. Historic St Albans. 1946.

Swinson, A. The Quest for Alban. 1971.

Thurston, H. S. The Urban regions of St Albans. 1954.

Toms, E. The Story of St Albans. rev. ed. 1975.

Toms, E. St Albans as it was. 1973.

Wheeler, R. E. M. *and* T. V. Verulamium; a Belgic and two Roman cities. 1936.

The Abbey
Buckler, I. C. *and* C. A. A History of the architecture of the Abbey Church of St Alban. 1847.
Carr, J. W. C. The Abbey Church of St Albans. 1877.
Chapple, J. A Short history of the Abbey Church of St Alban. 1882.
Langley, W. *publisher.* An account of the St Albans Abbey, and the churches of St Michael, St Peter and St Stephen. 1869.
Levett, A. E. Studies in manorial history. 1938.
Neale, J. The Abbey Church of St Alban, Hertfordshire. 1877.
Neale, J. Architectural notes on St Albans Abbey. 1877.
Newcome, P. The History of the ancient and royal foundation called the Abbey of St Alban. 1795.
Nicholson, H. J. B. The Abbey of St Alban. 1856.
Williams, L. F. R. History of the Abbey of St Alban. 1917.

One hundred and forty years ago, St Albans looked like this; enough has survived to bridge the centuries of this great city's long and distinguished past.

Index

Subscribers

Presentation copies

1 HM QUEEN ELIZABETH THE QUEEN MOTHER
2 St Albans City & District Council
3 The Earl of Verulam
4 The Right Reverend The Bishop of St Albans
5 St Albans City Library
6 St Albans Museums

7 Dr Elsie Toms
8 Clive Birch
9 Mrs Jean Hind
10 Geo. Ordish
11 James A. Howlett
12 Miss B. Duplock
13 Alan and Pauline O'Dell
14 H. MacDonald
15 Mrs L. Littlejohns
16 Peter J. E. Brunning
17 Mrs M. Mercer
18 C. M. Taylor
19 Mr & Mrs E. J. Heathman
20 W. R. Batchelor
21–32 Hertfordshire Library Service, Headquarters
33–42 Hertfordshire Library Service, St Albans
43–49 Bibliographic Unit, Welwyn Garden City
50 L. A. Howard
51 Mr & Mrs J. A. Kneath
52 Miss N. J. Wydell
53 J. P. Cooke
54 Dr J. W. Harding
55 Mrs B. Spear
56 Mrs E. V. Dowsett
57 Dr M. Charlesworth
58 Miss Mary Hanson
59 R. H. Wilson
60 Jon Ladbrooke
61 P. J. Clarke
62, 63 A. C. Slimmon
64 Mrs G. P. Buchanan
65 Mrs A. M. Bailey
66 Mrs Diana R. Deans
67 A. S. Moody
68 Richard Ames
69 Mrs Gene Peyton Jones
70 Alfred John Ottley
71 Mrs J. S. A. Rose
72 T. W. Stone
73 Mrs M. W. J. Grummitt
74 Mrs Sue Clendon
75 G. A. Dunk
76 Mr & Mrs G. J. Jex
77 Mrs M. Ashby
78 F. M. Redington
79 Richard E. Stagg
80 D. G. Lund
81 M. Downes
82 Mrs G. Short
83 C. H. Gansert
84, 85 A. Lawson
86 T. J. Evans
87 W. J. Underwood
88 D. F. Hardman
89 John B. Clark
90 Mr & Mrs N. Grenyer
91 John G. E. Cox
92 D. M. Miller
93 J. A. B. Townsend
94 R. Seymour
95, 96 Miss R. Graham
97 Mrs Eileen Akerman
98 Mrs H. Sweet
99 H. J. Vincent JP
100 Mrs Sheila Kendall
101 J. A. D. Hall
102 C. Liversedge
103 Miss S. J. Messenger
104 Dr Dorothy J. Marsden
105 A. G. Ingledew
106 James Frew
107 R. A. Seabrook
108 D. L. Jones
109 Verulam School
110 John Mathews
111 J. R. Brittin
112 S. J. Beck
113 Mrs M. Hutchinson
114 L. & K. A. Sowry
115 T. W. Jones
116 J. F. Price
117 James Evans
118 M. S. Harland
119 N. L. Kent
120 Mrs M. Duncanson
121 Mrs Ann Deyermond
122 J. Nursaw
123 Mrs. E. M. Bennett
124 Anthony Bryant
125 Peter Lawrence
126 M. B. Baxter
127 H. B. Lock
128 Mrs S. P. Bury
129 David Hance
130 Anne Marie Kelly
131 Richard Thrale
132 Miss M. Cooke
133 J. W. Peters
134 G. H. Turner
135 J. Henry Bryden-Smith
136 D. R. Owen
137 M. Tomkins
138 David M. Jacobs
139 Y. McLaird
140 Clifford H. Smith
141 Mr Bishop
142 Mrs Rosslyn French
143 Mrs J. M. Kenworthy
144 J. Gallons
145 R. E. Underwood
146 M. Horan
147–159 Hertfordshire Schools Library Service
160 P. Cooper
161 D. F. Kiff
162 P. J. Williams
163 Rowena Middle
164 Mrs B. Stockwell
165 B. King
166 S. R. Fordham
167 E. G. Cox
168 W. A. Mellors
169 Mrs D. M. Brittain
170 Mrs A. Gunner
171 Mrs J. R. Parker
172 G. Whitehead
173 J. Raxworthy
174 R. Jewell
175 I. Wharton
176 M. J. Thomas
177 J. A. Dawson
178 Mrs R. Mitchell
179 Mr & Mrs R. C. Chalk
180 J. C. Everett
181 Mrs S. Culling
182 Mr & Mrs J. Taylor
183 P. J. Seaman
184 Mrs M. Richardson
185 Mrs A. C. Potter
186 R. Williams
187 Mrs P. M. Jervis
188 M. A. Malet
189 A. H. Dickenson
190 J. W. Lengley
191 R. J. S. Jackson
192 Mrs J. G. Hiscocks
193 G. R. Mogg
194 Mrs D. L. Eldred
195 Mrs F. M. T. Hodge
196 A. Johnson
197 P. Garnham
198 Miss Sanora Mercer
199 Ernest Gordon
200 R. N. Hall
201 P. S. Elliston
202 Mr Alcock
203 K. J. Wheaton
204 Mrs G. Hutchen
205 Mr & Mrs J. D. Duggan
206 Marie Townsend
207 G. J. Baker
208 Alfred J. Gentle
209 Geraldine D. Sauvage
210 R. Jefferies
211 Dorothy G. Dickerson
212 Mrs Barbara Gibson
213 M. J. Scott
214 John Watson
215 D. Trueman
216 Mr Attfield
217 Mrs L. E. Booth
218 Mrs Sharpe
219 Mrs J. M. Reavell
220 Muriel Thresher
221 D. W. Foscoe
222 Mr & Mrs W. A. Dodd
223 J. F. Sawson, Headmaster, Beaumont School
224 Michael R. Frodsham
225 Mrs R. E. Henn
226 A. E. Ranger
227 Mr & Mrs Barry
228 Mr & Mrs R. J. Davies
229 R. Gribbell
230 Michele Thrussell
231 Miss D. A. Mock
232 D. R. Shannon
233 Michael J. Pugh
234 J. A. Cooper
235 J. Wooding
236 K. Hornby
237 Major David Gape, MBE, DL, JP
238 Mrs K. B. Nicolson
239–249 Hertfordshire Library Service, West Division
250–252 Bibliographic Unit, Welwyn Garden City
253 John Beaumont
254 Mrs Marjorie D. Barratt

255 John T. Bristow
256 Mrs V. L. Thomas
257 Simon Lindley
258 W. G. Walmsley
259 The Lord Aldenham
260, 261 The Right Reverend The Bishop of St Albans
262 Geoffrey Kinglake
263 Norman Morley Bailey
264 J. A. Bond
265 John H. Penton
266 H. P. Sharpe
267 Miss Veronica Little
268 J. G. Bromfield
269 Rhodri Pazzi-Axworthy
270 Arianrhod Pazzi-Axworthy
271 Pamela Elizabeth Coburn
272 J. R. Kell, CBE
273 Mrs Hodge
274 Major S. Whitbread
275 Miss L. L. Upton
276 Alfred White Franklin
277 Ann Grizel Franklin
278 Miss M. Brookes
279 Humphry Whitbread
280 Peter M. Gimson
281 R. H. Lyne
282 Mrs Gladys Clark
283 Raymond W. Birch, CBE
284 Miss Winifred Beal
285 The Rt Revd The Bishop of Hertford
286 Canon P. R. Morgan
287 W. B. Sharland
288 Harman Munro
289 C. A. Pain
290 Sheila Hughes-Parry
291 Peter Dent Smith
292 Miss M. R. Brackett
293 Dr K. R. Norton
294 Robert Rendell
295 Mrs K. M. Moody
296 Mrs C. Ball-Kasanis
297 C. E. Peskett
298 H. F. Jones
299 Alan David Roper
300 Mrs M. Tatlock
301 Mrs P. J. Ransom
302 J. E. Clements
303 E. Godwin
304 Miss M. E. Gibbs, MA, FZS
305 Hatfield & District Archaeological Society
306 Mrs M. A. Roemmele
307 A. F. Rushporth
308 Joan Speller
309 E. J. G. Balley
310 H. J. J. King
311 Miss M. Harrington
312 D. E. Baker
313 Mrs J. E. Covey-Crump
314 L. A. Turtle
315 R. T. King
316 H. W. Mathew
317 A. M. Foster
318 Mrs S. Presky
319 Leonard G. Walker
320, 321 Miss K. W. Buckland
322 Dr M. E. Yapp
323 Colin Smart
324 I. E. Anthony
325 Miss D. Gibbons
326 Verulamium & City Museum
327 Dr Ronald E. Wilson
328 R. W. Messer
329 Donice Nayda
330 G. W. Bruton
331 Bertram Mycock
332 Mrs J. E. Baughn
333 Mrs R. Willson
334 Mrs J. Day
335 Miss E. J. Du Cane
336 John Robbins
337 Dr C. R. Jones, OBE
338 J. M. Warbis
339 S. D. Frearson
340 Mrs S. M. Baxendine
341 Alice Ivy Baker
342 Mrs S. Palmer
343 Mrs A. Byrom
344 Julia Watts
345 L. W. F. Stokes
346 Mrs S. Muston
347 C. C. Jones
348 Rev W. J. A. Turner
349 J. E. & D. Carey
350 Ian Bassham
351 E. A. Howes
352 Michael Hymas
353, 355 D. I. Moor
356 P. J. Schofield
357 J. S. Baldwin
358 J. S. Woodcock
359 G. C. Olney
360 Miss R. E. Simmons
361 Mrs M. E. Hudson
362 Derek Nash
363 Alban Pearson
364 A. Boothroyd
365 D. F. Kalabza
366 M. Williamson
367 Mrs C. A. Ambler
368 Brian Bailey
369 Mrs Braybrook
370 Ian R. Lee
371 Mrs M. J. Avison
372 A. Fordy
373 Miss J. T. de Marney
374 Mr & Mrs H. M. J. Ramshaw
375 Duncan Spence
376 Kenneth H. M. Curtis
377 F. G. W. Jones
378 L. I. Varty
379, 380 A. T. Collins
381 Suzanne Cranley
382 The Library, St Albans College of Further Education
383 Peter John Green
384 Barbara Humphreys
385 Miss E. Sheppard
386 Peter Wood
387 Mrs Lorna Wang
388 R. L. Helmore
389 Mr & Mrs Denis L. Hoy
390 Frank William Neale, MIEE, C.Eng.
391 Geoffrey Smith
392, 393 Eversheds
394 Wooley and Weston
395 Tom Graham
396 J. F. Mason
397 F. A. A. Murfet
398 Mrs Audrey Wadowska
399 J. A. J. Walker
400 John T. Scoote
401 M. T. Anderson
402 Grove Hill School
403 Miss Christine Blow
404 J. R. Alcock
405 Peter Bell
406 T. J. Beardsmore
407 Tony Lammiman
408 A. D. McWhirr, BSc, MA, FSA
409 Miss S. Price
410 Frank Pinnock
411 R. N. Clark
412 Rae Virginia Bloxham
413 W. J. Parker
414 Elizabeth Bird
415 Miss R. M. Thicknesse
416 Thelma E. Vernon
417 Dr G. H. Wyatt
418 Peter Chard
419 Malcolm Read
420 David Read
421 F. R. Smith
422 Stephen and Vicki Wegg-Prosser
423 Valerie C. Baskwill
424 R. F. Humphries
425 K. Clifton

Remaining names unlisted.

ENDPAPERS: FRONT—Map of St Albans, Stukeley, 1721.

BACK—Plan of Tourists' St Albans by Spendlove. (Courtesy of City and District Council)

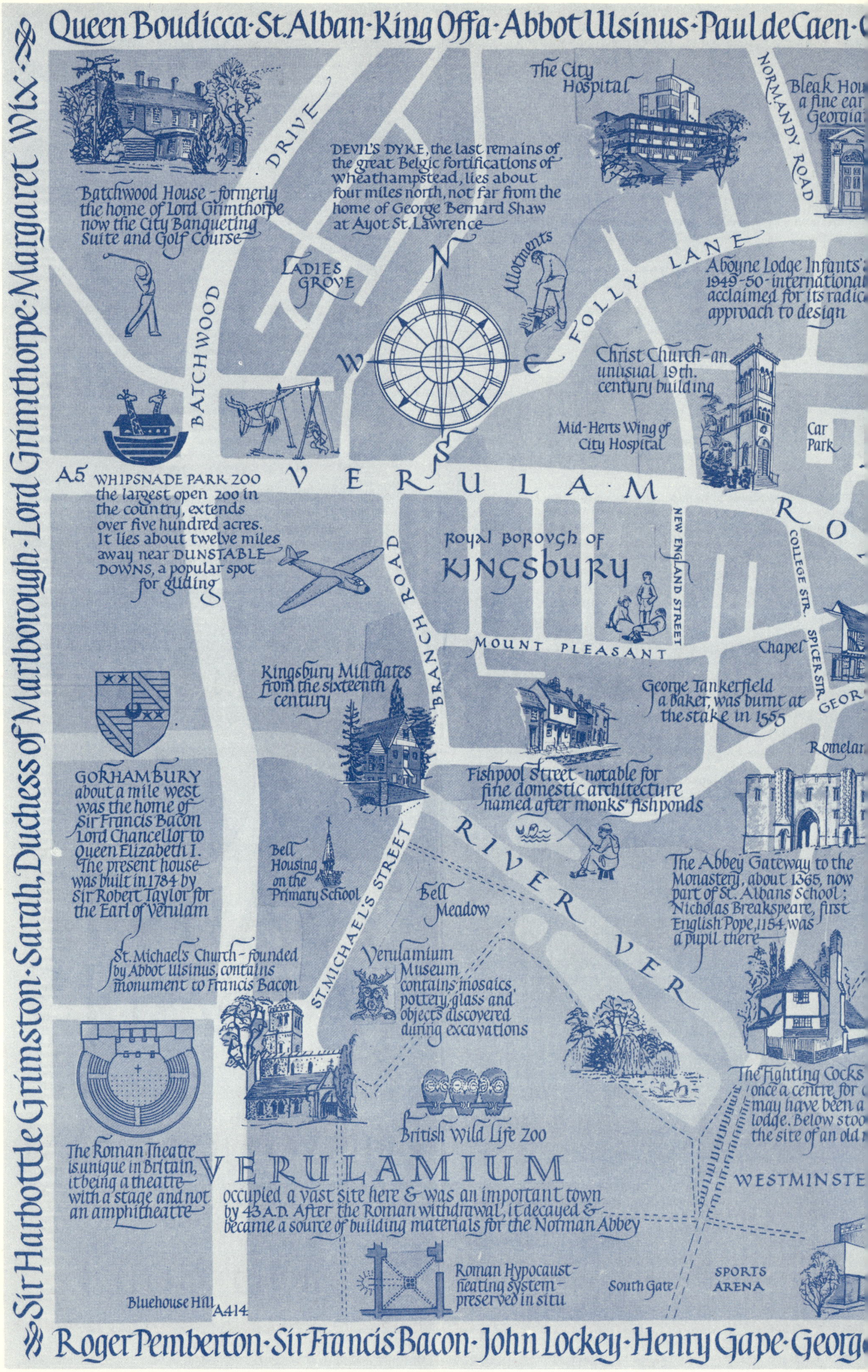

Queen Boudicca · St. Alban · King Offa · Abbot Ulsinus · Paul de Caen ·
Sir Harbottle Grimston · Sarah, Duchess of Marlborough · Lord Grimthorpe · Margaret Wix ·
Roger Pemberton · Sir Francis Bacon · John Lockey · Henry Gape · Georg
Batchwood House – formerly the home of Lord Grimthorpe now the City Banqueting Suite and Golf Course
DRIVE
BATCHWOOD
LADIES GROVE
DEVIL'S DYKE, the last remains of the great Belgic fortifications of Wheathampstead, lies about four miles north, not far from the home of George Bernard Shaw at Ayot St. Lawrence
The City Hospital
NORMANDY ROAD
Bleak Hou a fine ear Georgia
Allotments
FOLLY LANE
Aboyne Lodge Infants' 1949-50 - international acclaimed for its radic approach to design
N
W
E
S
Christ Church - an unusual 19th. century building
Mid-Herts Wing of City Hospital
Car Park
A5
WHIPSNADE PARK ZOO the largest open zoo in the country, extends over five hundred acres. It lies about twelve miles away near DUNSTABLE DOWNS, a popular spot for gliding
VERULAM ROAD
BRANCH ROAD
Royal Borough of KINGSBURY
NEW ENGLAND STREET
COLLEGE STR.
SPICER STR.
MOUNT PLEASANT
Chapel
GEOR
Kingsbury Mill dates from the sixteenth century
George Tankerfield a baker, was burnt at the stake in 1555
Romelan
GORHAMBURY about a mile west was the home of Sir Francis Bacon Lord Chancellor to Queen Elizabeth I. The present house was built in 1784 by Sir Robert Taylor for the Earl of Verulam
Fishpool Street - notable for fine domestic architecture named after monks' fishponds
RIVER VER
Bell Housing on the Primary School
ST. MICHAEL'S STREET
Bell Meadow
The Abbey Gateway to the Monastery, about 1365, now part of St. Albans School; Nicholas Breakspeare, first English Pope, 1154, was a pupil there
St. Michael's Church - founded by Abbot Ulsinus, contains monument to Francis Bacon
Verulamium Museum contains mosaics, pottery, glass and objects discovered during excavations
The Fighting Cocks once a centre for may have been a lodge. Below stoo the site of an old
British Wild Life Zoo
The Roman Theatre is unique in Britain, it being a theatre with a stage and not an amphitheatre
VERULAMIUM occupied a vast site here & was an important town by 43 A.D. After the Roman withdrawal, it decayed & became a source of building materials for the Norman Abbey
WESTMINSTE
Roman Hypocaust - heating system - preserved in situ
South Gate
SPORTS ARENA
Bluehouse Hill
A414